From the moment the first window is opened on the advent calendar until the last bow is untied on Christmas morning, the holiday season is filled with joy, tradition, anticipation and giving. When you *give* something that is homemade, you are giving more than a present—you are giving something money can't buy...a gift of yourself. Once you experience the delight found in creating and personalizing the season's festivities, new traditions will emerge. It is our hope that this book will inspire you to give of yourself. May you make this season your season of giving.

happy holidays!

Making Memories

contents

CHAPTER 1 | home décor   6

CHAPTER 2 | ornaments   14

CHAPTER 3 | homemade gifts   22

CHAPTER 4 | neighbor gifts   34

CHAPTER 5 | party ideas   46

CHAPTER 6 | children's projects   56

CHAPTER 7 | tags and wrapping   66

CHAPTER 8 | advent calendars   78

CHAPTER 9 | cards & cardholders   86

CHAPTER 10 | scrapbook pages, traditions   102
             and memories

The famous Christmas carol "Deck the Halls" invites listeners to adorn their homes with festive decorations. Most families trim their homes with traditional decorations such as a Christmas tree, wreaths and garland, but other items can add just as much holiday cheer. Use the ideas in this chapter to craft new additions to your holiday décor.

DECORATED CANDLES | BY HEIDI SWAPP

CHRISTMAS CAROL & SWAPP FAMILY CANDLE

1. Photocopy music or photos onto regular printer paper.

2. Trim the paper so it's no taller than the candle.

3. Affix the paper to the candle with straight pins.

4. With an embossing gun, heat the candle until the wax saturates and melts completely through the paper. Remove the pins.

5. Embellish the candle with ribbons, charms or other notions.

NOEL CANDLE

1. Wrap various ribbons around a candle.

2. Attach Alphabet Charms with adhesive dots.

PEACE CANDLE

1. Glue pressed leaves on a candle. Coat with a decoupage medium.

2. Adorn with ribbon and a mini tag.

BELIEVE CANDLE

1. Cut canvas to fit around a candle.

2. Stamp "believe" on the canvas with StazOn ink.

3. Set a snap on the canvas.

4. Pin embellished canvas to the candle.

5. Heat with an embossing gun until the wax saturates and melts completely through the canvas.

Adhesive: Mod Podge, Plaid
Alphabet charms, eyelet word, snap and stick pins: Making Memories
Alphabet stamps: PSX Design
Stamping ink: StazOn, Tsukineko
Tag: American Tag
Other: Canvas, foliage, photocopies of music and photos, pillar candles, pressed flowers, ribbon and trim

Candles always represent the holiday season to me. Since I was young, I have loved a mantel lined with pine boughs and burning candles. I love how easy these *candles* are to make! They complement each other and look beautiful together. They would also make fun gifts.

Stockings are my most favorite part of Christmas morning. When I was little, I remember finding a little bottle of perfume wrapped as a gift in the very bottom of my *stocking*. I remember how exciting it was to have finished opening all of my gifts, only to find one last surprise! So at our home, we open gifts and save our stockings for last. You never know what little surprise it may hold!

STOCKINGS

1. Sketch a stocking onto paper to determine the size you want. Cut out and pin to your base fabric.

2. Cut out the fabric to form the front of your stocking.

3. Cut a piece of Warm & Natural batting to back the fabric.

4. Cut two pieces of canvas. These pieces will create a sturdy backing for the stocking. (They don't need to be perfect because you want the edges to be a little rough to maintain a primitive look.)

5. Tea-dye muslin and allow to dry.

6. Trace a child's hand onto the muslin with a fabric pen.

7. Stitch the hand shape and rinse out the pen marks.

8. Paint the Eyelet Letters and Metal Words with acrylic paint. Seal with a matte-finish acrylic sealer.

9. Glue the letters and words into place, then stitch them to the stocking.

10. Pin everything else in place before stitching so you can rearrange if necessary.

11. Layer the top fabric, batting and two pieces of canvas, and top stitch around the outside edges. Be sure to leave the top open if you want them to be functional.

Variation: A creative way to display these stockings would be to have each child photographed with Santa. Develop the photos in a sepia tone, then frame in a 5"x 7" black frame. Hang each child's picture directly above his or her sock and hang the word "JOY" above the photographs.

Acrylic sealer: Decorative Crafts
Batting: Warm & Natural
Buttons, eyelet letters, metal words and scrapbook stitches: Making Memories
Curtain rod: Traditions
Paint: Delta
Wooden words: Twelve Timbers
Other: Canvas, fabric quarters and muslin

PRIMITIVE STOCKINGS | BY KRIS STANGER

BELIEVE PILLOW & TABLE RUNNER | By Jennifer Jensen

I have enjoyed making pillows and table runners to use as a holiday decoration and as gifts for my friends. To me, "believe" is a word that captures the feeling of Christmas: if you believe in Christmas and the Christmas spirit, magical things will happen. So *stitching* that word on the pillow helps me remember what the holiday season is all about.

PILLOW

1. Sketch the word "Believe" onto black fabric with a white colored pencil.

2. Stitch over the pencil lines with Scrapbook Stitches.

3. Use assorted fabrics to make a patchwork design for the pillow top.

4. After the front is complete, set Eyelet Shapes on the fabric just as you would on paper.

5. To make the back of the pillow and to allow for insertion of the pillow form, cut two pieces of fabric the same width as the front and about two-thirds the length of the front. Hem one of the longer sides of each piece, then lay the pieces right sides together with the back pieces overlapping one another. Stitch around all four sides, including fringe in the side seams.

6. Turn the pillow top right side out and insert a pillow form.

Eyelet shapes and scrapbook stitches:
Making Memories
Gold fabric: Fabricut
Gold fringe: Wrights
Pillow form: Create-a-Craft
Other: Burgundy fabric, button and velvet

TABLE RUNNER

1. Randomly piece together assorted fabrics in a crazy-patch design.

2. Cut a table-runner shape from the patched fabric.

3. Randomly stitch Charmed Stars and black beads to the top. Set Eyelet Shapes the same way you set them on paper.

4. After completing the top piece, cut a bottom piece and sew right sides of both pieces together, including a tassel on each end. Leave an opening on one side for turning. Turn the runner inside out and hand stitch the opening closed.

Adhesive: Metal Glue, Making Memories
Beads, charmed stars, eyelet shapes, eyelet words
and scrapbook stitches: Making Memories
Gold fabric: Fabricut
Rhinestone: Westrim
Tassels: Wrights
Other: Fabric, large beads and trim

WINTER MEMORIES | By Jennifer Jensen

WINDOW FRAME

1. Collect objects that represent your favorite winter memories. Collage the items behind the glass.

2. Paint the snowflakes with acrylic paint and seal with a satin-finish fixative. Glue rhinestones to the snowflakes. Dangle them from nails nailed into the top of the window frame.

3. Cut old book covers to frame the pictures and to make the poinsettia.

4. Rub the edges of the poinsettia with an inkpad.

5. Sew an X over the leaves to secure, then sandwich them between pink tulle. Machine stitch over the top of all the layers.

6. Spray paint the Shaped Eyelets, then spray with a fixative. Add to the collage.

7. Apply Simply Stated rub-ons to the glass.

Adhesive: Metal Glue, Making Memories
Alphabet page pebbles, defined stickers, eyelet charms, eyelet shapes, funky with fiber and simply stated rub-ons: Making Memories
Embossed card: Merrimack Publishing Corp.
Embossing enamel: Ultra Thick Embossing Enamel, Suze Weinberg
Fixative: Krylon
Paint: Delta
Paper: Frances Meyer
Rhinestones: Westrim
Santa sticker: John Grossman
Sheet music: Ideals
Silk ribbon: Bucilla
Spray paint: Rust-Oleum
Stamping ink: Stampin' Up!
Other: Fabric, old book covers, rhinestone button, safety pins, small hooks, tag, tin ceiling tile, tin snowflake, tulle, vintage lace and vintage postcards

I have an affinity for old windows. I just love them! Several pictures in my home are even framed with old *windows*. So I thought a clever way to preserve winter memories—photos, memorabilia, found objects, etc.—would be to collage them in a window frame. Collecting the items brought back Christmas memories, and I had fun arranging them to create a special holiday decoration.

Decorating a tree can be a magical event. It's amazing how a plain tree can be transformed into a delightful feast for the eyes. The lights draped around the branches provide a lustrous backdrop for the ornaments that are hung on the boughs. Whether you make a new ornament to keep for yourself or make one to give away, the ideas in this chapter are sure to add flourish when trimming the tree.

METAL STARS | BY JULIE TURNER

METAL ORNAMENTS

1. Create a five-pointed star pattern from paper. For a quick and easy star, use the "5-Pointed Star In One Snip" found on the Betsy Ross website (www.ushistory.org/betsy/flagstar).

2. Tape the star pattern over medium-weight pewter sheet metal. Cut out.

3. Using a ruler and stylus, score fold lines from the inside corners to the center. Turn the star over and score fold lines from the points to the center. If you want a design in the metal, punch the metal before folding.

4. Carefully fold on the scored lines to create a 3-D star. Use a ruler to help make neat folds.

5. Spray paint the stars with glossy white paint and use sandpaper to rough them up.

6. Create a hanger with twisted wire strung with beads.

Variation: Hang two stars together to create a double-sided star. Punch holes in the points of the stars. Loop silver thread through the holes and string beads on the thread, tying a knot at the end.

Eyelet charm, jump ring and wire: Making Memories
Pewter sheet metal: American Art Clay Co.
Spray paint: Krylon
Other: Beads and thread

These were so much fun to make, from learning how to cut a five-pointed star with only one snip of the scissors to easily cutting metal and bending it into a three-dimensional shape. Because the *stars* are quick to make, there is plenty of time to experiment with variations. Try different colors of paint, change the size of the star, rubber stamp a design on the surface or embellish with unusual trinkets. Metal stamps could be used to imprint a name or other Christmas greeting to make a personalized gift.

ORNAMENT WITH CRYSTALS | By Erin Terrell

CRYSTAL ORNAMENT

1. Place small adhesive dots on a pre-frosted glass ornament.

2. Add eyelet backings to the adhesive dots.

3. Add crystals to the centers of the silver eyelet rims. Voila! Studded crystal accents!

4. Hang the ornament with white ribbon.

Crystals and eyelet backings: JewelCraft
Ribbon: Offray

Some of my most cherished holiday memories involve trimming the tree with my family. We'd all gather around to decorate it and reminisce over the ornaments. It seemed like every ornament had a story. We've had some good laughs trying to figure out some of our creations we made as children. Thankfully, my ornament-making attempts have improved since those days, and I love to give *handmade* ornaments as gifts. This ornament is a simple, yet elegant, ornament to make, and your recipient won't have to guess what it is!

I thought it might be fun to pull out the best

of the old Christmas and winter photos to use on

ornaments to adorn a "family tree." My hope is

that the *photo* ornaments, hung

from a tabletop-size Christmas tree, will be a

conversation piece and catalyst for my family to

connect and share memories from years past. I

included heritage and current photos, which

I changed to black and white to create a more

uniform look. The year the photo was taken is

stamped on the ribbon.

GLASS ORNAMENTS

1. Photocopy a photo onto Lazertran, an image transfer material that works like a decal.

2. Soak the paper in water and adhere the decal to a pre-cut glass shape.

3. Stamp the year the photo was taken onto the ribbon.

4. Thread ribbon through the hole in the glass and wrap the ends together with wire.

5. Hang a snowflake Wire Shape from the ribbon with a safety pin.

Glass: Provo Craft
Magnetic alphabet stamps, safety pin,
snowflake wire shapes and wire: Making Memories
Stamping ink: StazOn, Tsukineko
Transfer paper: Lazertran
Other: Ribbon

GLASS PHOTO ORNAMENTS | By Julie Turner

HANGING STARS | By Jennifer Jensen

PAPER ORNAMENTS

1. Cut a primitive star shape out of cardboard and tissue paper. Cut the tissue paper star slightly larger than the cardboard star.

2. Apply Mod Podge to the cardboard star, then lay tissue paper on top.

3. Apply Mod Podge to top of the tissue paper. Jennifer likes the tissue paper to appear crinkly and wrinkled.

4. Set an eyelet at the top after the star is dry. Hang with ribbon.

Adhesive: Mod Podge, Plaid
Eyelets: Making Memories
Other: Cardboard, ribbon and tissue paper

I wanted to find a quick and simple way to create a fantastic ornament. I knew I wanted to *hang* stars from the ceiling at different lengths around the angel at the top of my tree. I also wanted to hang them from other places in my home. It is such a wonderful feeling when you walk into my family room at night and see twinkling lights and stars dangling from the ceiling.

Christmas is the perfect time to acknowledge those who add so much to our lives—from a sibling, to the friend who took your carpool turn, to the hairstylist who gave you a new look. In this chapter, the artists have designed novel ideas for creative homemade gifts that will be truly appreciated. These one-of-a-kind creations will be the perfect "thank you" for those most dear to you.

Krum Kage

Every Christmas, Mom makes these Norwegian cone-shaped cookies. She uses a special krum kage iron that imprints a design on the cookies.

3 eggs, beaten
1 cup sugar
½ cup cream, whipped
1 ½ cups flour
1 teaspoon vanilla
½ cup melted butter, folded in

Mix all ingredients, bake in iron and roll while hot.

Grandma Opal taught Sarah and Jillian to make krum kage (Norwegian for cream cakes) in 2002.

Come, Lord Jesus, be our guest, and let thy gifts to us be blessed. Amen.

When we were children, we said this prayer before each meal.

appetizers · side dishes · breads · desserts · soups & salads

family

FAMILY RECIPE BOX | BY JULIE TURNER

One of my favorite childhood memories is gathering around the dinner table, laughing and

conversing while enjoying delicious meals prepared by my mom. It's probably due to Mom's

example that we have become an entire family of cooks. I thought it might be fun to create a

family recipe box for each of my siblings as a Christmas gift. The box contains Mom's most

memorable *recipes*, favorites from my grandmothers, and recipes that are my

siblings' specialties. A copy of our childhood mealtime prayer is inside the box lid.

RECIPE BOX

1. Spray a wooden box with several coats of white semi-gloss paint. Lightly sand the box between each coat to keep the surface smooth.

2. When the final coat is dry, sand all the edges and corners to give the box a slightly worn look.

3. Give the box a patina and luster finish by rubbing it with paste wax. Apply a thin coat of paste wax with a smooth cloth, rubbing in a circular motion. After the paste has dried enough to look clouded, buff the waxed surface with a smooth, clean cloth. Repeat the process until you have three or four coats of wax. (Paste wax is available at home improvement stores.)

4. To decorate the box, adhere a photo to the top, then cover with a thin piece of glass. The easiest way to adhere the glass is with four tiny adhesive dots.

5. Hang a tag from a decorative snap attached to the front of the box.

6. Make copies of food-related family photos and cut them to recipe card size to make the category dividers. For a few of the dividers Julie scanned memory-evoking items such as a plate from her mom's china and the design from a favorite linen tablecloth. Back the photos with cardstock printed with journaling, and sandwich the plastic tab labels between the two layers. Secure with a snap.

7. All the cardstock Julie used was stained with walnut ink. And the recipes follow a simple format and were printed on the computer to save time.

Computer font: Georgia, WordPerfect
Paste wax: Howard Products
Plastic labels: Avery
Recipe cards: Esselite
Snaps and tag: Making Memories
Spray paint: Krylon
Unfinished wooden recipe box: Walnut Hollow
Other: Glass

COLLAGE-ART FRAME AND CHEERS BOX | By Stephanie McAtee

When giving a gift, I like to *personalize* it. I love to make the presentation as fun and unique as the gift itself. So the thought on this wine gift box is to give it with wine accessories inside, such as wine glasses, wine jewelry, a cork screw, a wine facts handbook, bottle stoppers, etc. The Italian memorabilia—café receipts, ticket stubs and wine labels—added the perfect elemental feel. I also personalized this frame by painting and adding collage elements.

FRAME

1. Brush a gold accordion frame with acrylic paint, allowing some of the gold to show through.

2. Embellish the frame with a variety of items to enhance your photos. For example, Stephanie made a homemade envelope to house a hand-written note.

3. Add journaling to the frame with Defined stickers, Metal Words, Eyelet Alphabet letters and Alphabet Page Pebbles.

4. Frame a photo with a Charmed Frame and layer it over another photo.

#2: FoofaLa
Adhesives: Diamond Glaze, JudiKins;
Mod Podge, Plaid
Alphabet page pebbles, charmed frame,
charmed photo corners, defined stickers,
eyelet alphabet, eyelet shape and metal word:
Making Memories
Paint: Americana
Paper: 7 Gypsies
Ribbon: Paper Source
Rubber stamp: Stampotique Originals
Watch face and nickel rectangle: 7 Gypsies
Other: Concho, date stamp and frame

BOX

1. Decoupage a plain pencil box with wine-related items.

2. Cut wine corks in half and adhere them to the top of the pencil box.

3. Use the corks as a "cork board," sticking Stick Pins into them to secure little tags and notes.

Alphabet charms, defined stickers, eyelet alphabet,
screw snap and stick pins: Making Memories
Bottle cap: Manto Fev
Cigar label and rubber stamp: Limited Edition
Rubber Stamps
Paint: Americana
Pen: EK Success
Other: Ephemera, found objects, jewelry piece,
lock and key, pencil box, Santa tag and wine corks

I chose to make my friend a stitched

sampler for a Christmas

gift. I didn't use traditional Christmas colors

because I wanted it to be something she could

leave up all year. What I love about samplers

is that you can choose just about any saying

or poem that is fitting for the recipient.

STITCHING

1. Sketch out a saying onto fabric with a washable fabric pen.

2. Stitch the saying with Scrapbook Stitches, then rinse out the pen marks.

3. Iron the fabric.

4. Paint heart Eyelet Shapes, then lightly rub antiquing gel over the top with your finger. Spray with an acrylic matte-finish spray to prevent the paint from peeling.

5. Stitch silk ribbon and striped fabric into place and add pearls through the stitches.

6. Wrap floss around the hearts and thread the floss through a button.

7. Affix the embellished hearts to the sampler with pop-dots.

FRAME

1. Paint a wooden frame.

2. When dry, lightly rub brown antiquing gel over the top.

3. Unevenly sand the surface to give it an antiqued appearance.

Acrylic sealer: Decorative Crafts
Antiquing gel and paint: Delta
Buttons: Dress It Up
Eyelet shapes and scrapbook stitches:
Making Memories
Frame: Homemade from baseboard trim
Pearls: Darice
Silk ribbon: Bucilla
Other: Sandcastle muslin and vintage fabric

TRUE FRIENDS SAMPLER | By Kris Stanger

EARRINGS AND GIFT BOX | By Sharon Lewis
CHARM BRACELET | By Heidi Swapp

EARRINGS AND GIFT BOX

1. Bend earring wire into an earring shape and slide on the ornament charms.

2. Hang the earrings on a square of oatmeal cardstock.

3. Layer a strip of torn cardstock and printed paper at the top.

4. Finish it off with a fiber bow.

5. To make the gift box, unfold a paper box, trace onto the back of red printed paper and cut out.

6. Cover the box with the printed paper.

7. Cut two squares of coordinating printed papers and mat each one with cardstock.

8. Adhere one square to the top and one square to the front of the box.

9. Stitch buttons to the center of each square.

10. Wrap fibers around the buttons and tie in a bow to close.

Buttons, charmed ornaments and funky with fiber: Making Memories
Earring wire: www.beadsgalore.com
Paper: Making Memories and Anna Griffin
Other: Box

CHARM BRACELET

Purchase a ready-made bracelet with chain-style links.

Using a 1/16" drill bit, drill a hole in the star and snowman charms.

Attach the charms to the bracelet with jump rings.

Connect a Washer Word to the bracelet with small bead chain.

Frame a photo or festive sentiment and attach with jump rings.

Bead chain, charms, jump rings and washer word: Making Memories
Ribbon: Offray
Other: Bracelet and frame

Christmas sweatshirts, glittery sweaters, jingle bell socks: Christmas is a fun time to dress up in festive attire! Another great way to add holiday *charm* to your attire is with Christmas earrings or bracelets. This jewelry, along with the card and gift box, is a simple holiday project and makes a perfect gift!

I grew up in South Carolina where snowy days were few and far between. Any dip in the thermometer was a good excuse for us to break out the hot *chocolate* and marshmallows! Now that I live in San Antonio, winter weather is even more unusual.

With this tray and coaster set, I hope to carry on my hot chocolate traditions with my family.

I made this set in a vintage style so it will last many years.

TRAY

1. Transfer the Santa Claus images onto canvas by copying the image on a color copier either in color or black and white mode.

2. Place the sticky side of a laminate sheet over the copied image. Burnish or rub the laminate sheet to make sure all areas are well adhered.

3. Soak the image in a tub of warm water for two minutes, then remove.

4. Rub the paper off the laminate sheet. You will have to rub pretty hard and keep the paper wet. When all of the paper is rubbed off, you will have a sheet of laminate with the toner ink on it.

5. To get the laminate to stick to the canvas, paint a coat of Mod Podge on the canvas.

6. Place the transfer on the painted surface and let dry.

7. Brush another coat of Mod Podge over the top of the laminate to protect the fabric and images from spills.

8. Stitch around the edges of the canvas with Scrapbook Stitches.

9. Cut balsa wood into approximately 3½" squares. Cut square balsa dowels to rim the edges of the coasters. Adhere to wood squares with wood glue.

10. Paint the coasters and tray with black acrylic paint.

11. Once the paint has dried, paint a coat of matte-finish Mod Podge over the tray and coasters. Place the canvas on the tray and coasters, then add another coat of Mod Podge and allow to dry.

HOT CHOCOLATE BAG

1. Cut black paper to 12"x 6".

2. Lay your paper vertically and use a bone folder to make creases at the following measurements: 1½", 5½", 6", 7½", and 8".

3. Fold the crease at 1½" to make the flap.

4. Fold the other creases to create the bottom of the bag. (The bag will be open on two sides.)

5. Stamp "hot chocolate" on a sheet of off-white cardstock and add a coffee mug image.

6. Adhere to the front of the bag.

7. Punch holes in the top of the bag and tie shut with ribbon. (Tea stain or walnut ink black and white gingham to get a color to match your bag.)

Adhesive: Mod Podge, Plaid
Laminate sheets: Therm O Web
Paint: Americana
Paper: Sanook Paper Company
Santa Claus image: The Stock Solution
Scrapbook stitches: Making Memories
Stamping ink: Memories
Walnut ink: Postmodern Design
Rubber stamp: Just For Fun Rubber Stamps
Other: Balsa wood, balsa wood dowels,
canvas, mugs, ribbon and wooden tray

SANTA TRAY AND COASTERS | BY ERIN TERRELL

EMERGENCY PAMPERING KIT | By Lynne Montgomery

PAMPERING KIT

1. Design and print computer-generated labels on lightweight paper. When creating labels for the can, it is best to use lightweight paper instead of cardstock. The heavier your labels, the more difficult it will be for them to stick to the curved can.

2. Cut text into desired shapes, tear edges and lightly heat emboss with clear embossing enamel. Highlight the edges with an inkpad.

3. Layer the text, a piece of window screen and background paper. Attach text to background papers with eyelets, ribbon and fibers.

4. Ink and heat emboss flower Eyelet Charms. Attach with snaps.

5. Attach beads with Perfect Paper Adhesive and add other embellishments as desired.

6. Attach labels to the can using a strong binding adhesive.

7. Put contents inside and seal shut.

Variations: There are many variations of an emergency kit. Some examples might include a baby survival kit for first time parents, a newlywed kit, a scrapbooking kit or even a boredom kit for new retirees.

Adhesives: Metal Glue, Making Memories; Perfect Paper Adhesive, USArtQuest
Beads: Westrim
Computer fonts: CK Template and CK Typewriter, Creating Keepsakes; Amery, Jolt, Kabel Bk BT and Tabitha
Embossing enamel: Ultra Thick Embossing Enamel, Suze Weinberg
Embossing ink: Ranger Industries
Eyelet charms, eyelets, funky with fiber, ribbon charm, shaped clips and snaps: Making Memories
Paper: Making Memories and Karen Foster Design
Ribbon: Bucilla and May Arts
Stamping ink: Clearsnap
Other: Chocolate, emery board, face creams, foot lotion, foot scrub, lip color, nail enamel, paint can, pumice stone, soap, vitamin C, candle and window screen

I have been on the giving and receiving end of this gift, and both have brought a lot of happiness. A few years ago, a friend of mine gave me an "entertainment" kit filled with a Blockbuster gift card, popcorn and movie candy. It came at a time when finances were tight, so it was greatly appreciated! I wanted to return the favor to someone, so last Christmas another friend and I put together a "pampering/spa" version and anonymously gave it to three women who were in need of a *boost* in spirits. This gift is fun to put together and makes an ideal personalized gift.

Spread holiday cheer throughout your neighborhood by taking your neighbors a handmade gift. The gifts showcased in this chapter are not costly to make, but they will certainly show that you treasure your relationships. These gifts are also perfect to make ahead and have on hand for any unexpected occasion. So turn your home into Santa's workshop and start creating fabulous gifts every neighbor will love!

WHITE CHOCOLATE POPCORN | By Kris Stanger

POPCORN

1. Pop popcorn. You will use 1 tablespoon of oil to ½ cup of uncooked kernels. Kris swears by the Theatre II popcorn popper (stove top) and by Orville's Original popping corn, which produce large, fluffy popcorn. Air popped and microwave popcorn would also work.

2. Melt a one-pound bag of wafers.

3. Coat popcorn with melted wafers and spread out on waxed paper to cool.

4. Bag up the popcorn and decorate the bags.

Tag reads: "We hope Santa "pops" over to your home this holiday season!

Charmed photo corners and page pebbles: Making Memories
Computer font: 2Peas Tiny Tadpole, downloaded from www.twopeasinabucket.com
Paint: Delta
Paper: Making Memories and Bazzill Basics
Popcorn: Orville Redenbacher's Original Popcorn
Raffia: Berwick Industries
Vanilla-flavored wafers: Make n' Mold
Other: Large cellophane gusset bags

I received this *popcorn* as a gift from a friend about ten years ago. Since then, I have made it for just about every occasion. It is hard to find someone who doesn't love this popcorn. The wafers come in just about every color and in many flavors! Once I made a creamsicle blend with vanilla- and orange-colored and flavored wafers—it was to die for!

GALVANIZED MAGNETIC CHALKBOARD | By Stephanie McAtee

CHALKBOARD

1. Paint the galvanized steel with chalk paint.

2. Drill four holes at the top through which to tie a wire and bead-chain hanger.

3. Turn old coins, dominos and Charmed Frames into magnets.

4. Collage a large tag with assorted items, such as tags, keys and Alphabet Charms.

5. Add magnet strips to the back of the tag, frame and chalk.

6. Attach the tag to the wire hanger with ribbon.

Alphabet charms, bead chain, charmed frame, magnetic date stamp, staples and wire: Making Memories
Paint: Americana
Red alphabet and tag: FoofaLa
Other: Assorted ephemera, black chalk paint, bottle cap, chalk, domino, galvanized steel, magnet pieces, old coin and tape measurer

I enjoy giving gifts that people will utilize and won't get from someone else. I purchased a magnetic board from Sundance that hangs in my kitchen. I use it daily for notes, photos, etc. I also recently painted a small wall in my kitchen with *chalkboard* paint. I wrapped a long piece of wire around a piece of chalk and attached the other end of the wire to a nail in the wall. So I thought incorporating a magnetic board and a chalkboard would make a unique gift concept. I then added homemade magnets and a collaged tag.

This little star serves as a physical reminder

of the true spirit of Christmas — giving. The idea

is to do something nice for someone in your

family and leave the star on his or her bed. That

person then becomes "the recipient of goodness."

The recipient, in turn, does something nice

for someone else and passes on the *star*.

These little acts of kindness between family

members spread joy throughout your home.

This is an easy project to "mass produce,"

especially when you set it up assembly-line style.

Your older children can even help with several

of the steps.

STAR AND TAG

1. Trace the papier-mâché star on the back of printed paper.

2. Cut out ⅛" inside the line so it fits within the borders of the papier-mâché star. Set aside.

3. Paint the papier-mâché star with two coats of acrylic paint and shade the edges with ink.

4. Ink the edges of the paper star, then adhere it to the front of the papier-mâché star with Mod Podge.

5. Print the words "Blessed: recipient of goodness" on cream cardstock.

6. Trim "Blessed" to fit the oval tag. Using a light table, Sharon centered the tag under the text, traced around the rim with a stylus, cut out the word and glued it to the tag.

7. Ink the edges of the "recipient of goodness" word strip and apply to the front of the star along with the holly die cuts.

8. Paint the front of the oval tag with Mod Podge, then paint the front, back and sides of the star with Mod Podge.

9. When dry, attach the oval tag to the star with Scrapbook Stitches.

10. To make the accompanying tag, attach torn decorative paper to a tag.

11. Print the poem on regular paper first for spacing, then temporarily affix the tag over the top of the poem and run it through the printer again.

12. Ink the edges and paint the front and back with two coats of Mod Podge to make it sturdier.

13. Attach the tag to the star.

Adhesive: Mod Podge, Plaid
Die cuts: K & Company
Metal-rimmed tag and scrapbook stitches:
Making Memories
Paint: Delta
Paper: Amscan
Stamping ink: Clearsnap
Other: Papier-mâché star

Here's a magical Christmas star
With a tradition old and true
May it bring you warmth and love
From our home to you.

Now everyday 'til Christmas
Find someone in your home
And secretly do a deed of love
So your identity won't be known.

And when the secret act is done
Place the star upon their bed.
They in turn do a secret deed
For another, it is said.

And like the star so long ago
Lit the sky for all to see
May this star bring light & joy
To your sweet family.

Author Unknown

Blessed:
recipient of goodness

CHRISTMAS STAR | By Sharon Lewis

DECORATED FLORAL ALBUMS | By Rhonda Solomon

DECORATED ALBUMS

1. Hot glue a twig to the front of the album to make the tree trunk.

2. Using a craft knife, slightly hollow out a piece of the foam where it will fit over the trunk. Hot glue the foam piece to the cover. Rhonda used a small serrated knife to cut the foam into a triangle shape.

3. Hot glue the moss to the foam, making sure you "seal" around the edges.

4. Hot glue the roses into place.

5. Hot glue the ribbon to the insides of the cover and tie a bow to close.

Variation: Rhonda also created a moss-covered heart for an album. To create the same look, cut the foam into a heart shape, then follow steps three and four above.

Album: Making Memories
Desert foam: Create-a-Craft
Decorator moss: Luster Leaf Products
Miniature paper roses: Creative Elements
Other: Ribbon

I have kept a Christmas memories album for most of my marriage. I pack it away with our Christmas decorations, and it is one of our traditions to look at it and reminisce about years past. The kids always get a big kick out of what we looked like "pre-kids." I thought it would be fun to pass along this tradition, so last year I created *albums* and decorated the front to match the recipients' house or style. I simply made a master form on the computer and printed enough on cardstock to make the information pages. Each year, they will place a family photo on the form and write about their holiday season and what happened to them during the year.

This is a perfect neighbor gift: it's quick,

inexpensive and clever. The small, store-bought

liquid *soaps* are perfect for the

holiday season. Another alternative is to

purchase more upscale soap dispensers from

kitchen and bath stores and insert a more

general message.

SOAP BOTTLES

1. Create these customized liquid-soap dispensers with either pre-filled or empty liquid-soap dispensers.

2. If you are using pre-filled soap containers purchased from the grocery store, peel off the labels and use Un-Du to remove the sticky residue. Empty the soap into another container.

3. Cut a transparency to fit inside the bottle.

4. Embellish the transparency with your choice of products. Let your imagination run wild! For example, set Eyelet Words or affix brads to the transparency. However you choose to embellish, be sure you can roll up the transparency and get it through the opening.

5. Once your collage is complete, roll up the transparency and put it in the bottle.

6. Using tweezers or a skewer, arrange the transparency so it is right side up.

7. Refill the container with soap, making sure the transparency isn't laying against the front of the container.

8. Replace the pump so it's behind the transparency.

9. Tie ribbon and tags around the pump.

Variations: You could also stamp images on the transparency with StazOn ink or embellish with Simply Stated rub-ons.

Brads, eyelet words and metal-rimmed tags:
Making Memories
Stamping ink: StazOn, Tsukineko
Other: Alphabet stamps, liquid-soap dispensers,
liquid-soap refills, ribbon and transparencies

LIQUID SOAPS | By Heidi Swapp

NAPKIN RING HOLDERS | By Lynne Montgomery

NAPKIN RINGS

1. Glue two Charmed Frames together (wrong sides together).

2. When dry, slip a split ring around the frame along with an Eyelet Letter and beads.

3. Put a napkin through the center.

Adhesive: Metal Glue, Making Memories
Charmed frames and eyelet letters:
Making Memories
Other: Beads and split rings

My mother and sister are known in our family for having beautiful table arrangements. A large glass dome adorned my mother's table, and it was always filled with items representing a particular holiday. My sister lines her table with the perfect seasonal foliage and a plethora of beautiful candles. I am a "wanna-be table arranger."

I have always wanted to use decorative place-card holders labeling where guests will sit but never seem to find the time. So I loved the idea of placing initials on napkin *rings* in lieu of place-card holders. It's quick, easy and can be used over and over again. What a fun gift to share with your neighbors, as well!

December seems to be the perfect month to host or attend a holiday party. The spirit of the season encourages people to give of themselves and entertain others for an evening. If you've never hosted a party and would like to or if you want to add a twist to your annual celebration, consider hosting a cookie exchange, a caroling party or even a gingerbread-man party for little kids. Three artists share their ideas for a successful party—from the invitations to the party favors.

A CAROLING WE GO | BY HEIDI SWAPP

INVITATION

1. Cut a piece of red cardstock to 11¼"x 6". Score and fold 3¾" from the left and 3" from the right.

2. Fold the right-hand flap back 1¼" and stitch all the way around. Stamp "Fa La La La La" inside the sewn area. When making several invitations, Heidi suggests making them in stages: cut and fold all the cardstock, sew all the flaps, then do the stamping. When stamping, stamp all the "f's," all the "a's," all the "l's," etc.

3. Cut a piece of vellum to fit on the center panel. Rubber stamp sheet music on the vellum. Add a metal-rimmed tag with brads.

4. Sew the vellum piece to the center panel to create a pocket.

5. Print party information on cardstock and cut to fit inside the vellum pocket.

6. To create the closure, stitch one side of a swirl Shaped Clip to the left flap. The Shaped Clip will pivot and hold the invitation closed. Add a snowflake brad and ribbon over the top of the clip.

SONG BOOK

1. Cut 12"x 12" cardstock in half. With the 6"x 12" strip, create a tri-fold similar to the invitation. Score and fold 4½" from the left and 3½" from the right. This will be the cover of the song book.

2. Photocopy several Christmas carols or simply type up the words to the songs. The pages should be 4"x 6".

3. Insert the songs into the left-hand fold. Spiral bind the books at a copy store.

4. Fold the right flap back 1¼" like on the invitation. Sew around all sides, then stamp "Fa La La La La" in the sewn area.

5. Stamp the word "sing" on the black oval tag with white ink.

6. Punch an additional hole in the other end of the oval.

7. Thread ribbon through the holes and stitch down.

8. Use Velcro to keep flap closed.

I will be the first to admit I have a terrible singing voice and am anything but musical, but I do love singing Christmas *carols*. Having a caroling event is a great way to get families in the neighborhood together to celebrate the season.

HOT COCOA HOLDER

1. Cut 4" strips from 12"x 12" cardstock.

2. Fold one end over 1¾".

3. Using a ¾" circle punch, punch circles from black cardstock.

4. Place the hot chocolate packet in the fold. Place the black circle on top of the flap, then punch an ⅛" hole through all layers. Set with a snap.

5. Fold the other part of the cardstock over the hot chocolate packet and tuck underneath the small flap.

6. Embellish the front of the holder with rubber stamps and a snowflake brad.

Variation: You could also put hot apple cider packets inside the holder.

Alphabet stamps: PSX Design and
The Missing Link Stamp Company
Brads, magnetic date stamp, metal-rimmed
tags, ribbon, shaped clips and snaps:
Making Memories
Paper: Making Memories
Stamping ink: Clearsnap
Other: Christmas music, hot cocoa packets,
rubber stamp, vellum and Velcro

GINGERBREAD PARTY 1 | By Jennifer Jensen

What better way to get your kids excited about the holidays and let them enjoy time with friends than with a gingerbread party! There's nothing better than a bunch of giggling girls rolling out cookie dough, decorating *cookies* and chatting about the upcoming Christmas vacation and what they really need from Santa. They leave with a fresh plate of cookies for their family and enough goodies to make another batch at home.

INVITATION

1. Make a gingerbread-man pattern from paper, then trace it onto fabric. Cut out two pieces—one for the front and one for the back of the gingerbread man.

2. Sew the two pieces right sides together. Leave a little space open to insert the stuffing. Turn right side out, then stuff until full. Hand stitch the hole closed.

3. Finish the gingerbread man by sewing on the patch, eyes and buttons. Chalk the cheeks. Add greenery, cinnamon sticks and heart inside the patch.

4. For the actual invitation, sew a piece of muslin to cardstock.

5. Rubber stamp party information on the muslin.

6. Tie the recipe party invitation to the arm of the stuffed gingerbread man.

Alphabet stamps: PSX Design
Chalks: Craf-T Products
Cinnamon sticks: Grandma's Country Foods
Eyelet, eyelet charm, funky with fiber, magnetic date stamp, safety pin, scrapbook stitches and snap: Making Memories
Rick rack: Wrights
Silk ribbon: Bucilla
Stamping ink: Stampin' Up!
Stuffing: Polyfil
Other: Buttons, fabric and greenery

DRAW STRING BAG

1. Fold a rectangular piece of muslin in half and sew a straight seam on each side—right sides together.

2. Turn right side out, then fold a 2" cuff on the top of the bag. Set eyelets across the top about every 2" and string ribbon through the eyelets.

3. Rubber stamp the baking directions onto the bag, then put the bagged mix inside.

4. Pull the ribbon to cinch the bag shut.

Alphabet stamps: PSX Design
Cake and cookie mix: Betty Crocker
Eyelets, eyelet charms, metal rimmed tag: Making Memories
Other: Muslin and ribbon

UTENSIL BAG

1. Sew or buy canvas goodie bags.

2. Set an eyelet on each side of the bag, then tie fabric handles through the eyelets.

3. Fill with baking utensils the kids can use at the party and at home.

Baking utensils: Bella Bistro, Toysmith
Buttons, eyelets: Making Memories
Tube of frosting: Cake Mate
Other: Fabric and gingerbread-man cookie cutter

APRON

1. Buy a pre-made apron or create your own from canvas for each party guest.

2. Using Scrapbook Stitches, backstitch each guest's name on his or her apron.

3. Sew on heart and pockets.

Buttons, eyelets, scrapbook stitches and snaps:
Making Memories
Rick rack: Wrights
Other: Fabric and felt

FABRIC GARLAND

1. Find several pieces of coordinating fabrics. Tear the fabric into approximately 2" wide strips. Cut to desired length.

2. Cut a long piece of jute. The length will vary, depending on the area from which you would like to hang the garland. Loop the ends of the jute to hang the garland.

3. Tie the fabric strips to the jute, sliding them close together until you reach the end of the jute.

Jute: Wellington
Other: Fabric

GINGERBREAD MEN AND WOODEN HEARTS GARLAND

1. Paint wooden hearts with acrylic paint. Drill holes in the hearts and string two together with thin jute.

2. Trace gingerbread men onto brown paper and cut out.

3. Adorn with buttons, rick rack and heart snaps.

4. Paint on eyes and rub chalk over cheeks.

5. Set an eyelet at the top of each gingerbread man.

6. String thin jute through the eyelets of two gingerbread men.

7. Drape the hearts and gingerbread men over the fabric garland.

Buttons, eyelets, scrapbook stitches and snaps:
Making Memories
Chalk: Craf-T Products
Paint: Delta
Paper: Making Memories
Rick rack: Wrights
Wooden hearts: Robert's Crafts

GINGERBREAD PARTY 2 | By Jennifer Jensen

Clitter Clatter
Baking Tins
Cookie Cutters
Rolling Pin
Christmas Cookies
Let's begin!

yum   party

Warm Wishes !
to enjoy
with your
holiday treats

INSTRUCTION:
Combine butter, brown sugar...
10 minutes then add eggs, flour, baking...
at least 1 hour to firm. Then, roll into balls and bake at...
Remove from oven and place 1 under mint on each warm cookie...
for the mint to melt and then use a spoon to spread it around on to...

COOKIE EXCHANGE | By Lynne Montgomery

Hosting a cookie exchange is a quick and easy way to get a wide assortment of delicious

holiday treats. Invite family and friends to *bake* six dozen of their favorite holiday

cookie. Spend a delightful evening exchanging baked goods, recipes, and Christmas memories!

Exchanging cookies saves you time and money because you only have to concentrate on baking

one type of cookie.

OVEN MITT

1. For the oven mitt, adhere scrim to white torn cardstock with spray adhesive. Fray the edges of the material.

2. Print poem on vellum and attach with a pin.

3. Tear a small square of patterned paper and attach to lower left corner with an eyelet. Attach bead chain and metal-rimmed tag.

4. Wrap ribbon around the oven mitt and tie closed. Attach the poem with a Shaped Clip.

5. Fill the oven mitt with a mini rolling pin, a small cookie cutter and the invitation.

INVITATION

1. To create the invitation, tear a square of white cardstock and adhere green scrim to the bottom portion. Fray the edges.

2. Tear a piece of patterned paper and adhere to the top portion.

3. Set two eyelets, one on either side near the top. Run ribbon through the eyelets, forming a line from which to hang embellishments. Knot the ends.

4. Hang three Shaped Clips from the ribbon. On the center clip, attach a metal-rimmed tag with a snowflake charm. On the other two clips, attach squares of cardstock printed with text. Highlight the words with Page Pebbles. Use adhesive dots to keep the embellishments from sliding.

5. Mount the entire embellishment to the front of a card.

6. Print the details of your party on a separate square of cardstock and mount on the inside.

RECIPE CARD

1. For the recipe card, print the recipe on white cardstock, then mount on red. Attach to a 3"x 5" card, half covered with patterned paper and half covered with frayed scrim.

2. The party favor is a pillow-shaped box containing a packet of cocoa and tied with ribbon. For a sturdier box, use spray adhesive to adhere a thin piece of patterned paper to cardstock before die cutting the box.

Adhesive: Metal Glue, Making Memories
Bead chain, charmed snowflake, eyelets, metal-rimmed tags, page pebbles, shaped clips and stick pins: Making Memories
Computer fonts: CK Fresh, CK Jester, CK Pretty and CK Twilight, Creating Keepsakes; Amery
Paper: Susan Branch
Pin: Dritz
Vellum: Making Memories
Other: Cookie cutter, hot cocoa packets, mini rolling pin, oven mitt, pillow box, ribbon and scrim

It just seems like you have to go to a *party* on New Year's Eve! New Year's is a perfect time to reflect on the memories of the past year and to anticipate the future! Creating a time capsule is such a great way to capture both. Whether you make one as a group or as individuals, it's a perfect way to celebrate life and the people you love. The more creative you are at putting it together, the more fun it is to open!

INVITATION

1. Cut black paper into two 5"x 12" pieces.

2. Fold both pieces in half, leaving ½" overhang on the ends.

3. Use snowflake brads to bind the two pieces together.

4. To make the invitation double as a time capsule entry, adhere 10 mini envelopes to the inside. Write a question on the envelope and put a tag inside. The guest will write his or her thoughts about that question on the tag and return it to the envelope. All the invitations will be compiled into the time capsule and read at a later, pre-determined time.

5. Embellish the front of the card with a snowflake charm under a large vellum tag. Add ribbon to the binding.

6. Print instructions and party information on separate papers and secure to the inside with Shaped Clips.

CHAMPAGNE GLASSES

1. Apply Simply Stated Mini rub-ons to the glasses according to the directions on the package.

2. Embellish the stem with ribbon and a charm attached to bead chain with a jump ring.

CREATING A TIME CAPSULE

1. Ask participants to complete the tags found in their invitation and to bring them to the party.

2. Request that they bring other items that capture their lives at that time. Some suggestions would be photographs, a CD with favorite music or mementos which reflect their time of life.

3. That night, take photos and tape record or video tape interviews with each person and have them write a note to his or her future self. Include all these in the time capsule, which could be anything from a paint can to a treasure box.

4. Seal the container. Decide when it shall be opened again and note that date on the outside.

Bead chain, jump ring, metal-rimmed tag, shaped clips, simply stated mini and snowflake brads: Making Memories
Mini envelopes: Hero Arts
Ribbon: Midori
Small tag: American Tag
Snowflake charm: Embellish It!
Other: Champagne glasses and tag punch

NEW YEAR'S PARTY | By Heidi Swapp

Capturing the essence of childhood in a gift—through a child's handwriting, artwork or other personal touch—is truly priceless. Encourage the special child in your life to create gifts that will be meaningful to the recipient simply because he or she made them. Parents, grandparents, teachers and friends will be touched to receive a gift made by a child. So create a memory with a child while making gifts that will truly be treasured.

TRAVEL KIT | By Heidi Swapp

TRAVEL KIT

1. Purchase supplies—travel bottles, clear zipper travel bag, shampoo, etc.—in coordinating colors.

2. Choose artwork your child has created. It could be one image or a variety of images.

3. Scan them into the computer and re-size them to fit the bottles. Print, then cut into appropriate label sizes.

4. Draw a thin border around the perimeter of each label.

5. Run the labels through a Xyron machine and adhere to the bottles.

6. Place a piece of clear packing tape over the label to make it waterproof.

7. For the mouthwash, place one of the labels you created over the existing label.

8. To create a first-aid kit, gather the following items: Altoid tin, Band-Aids and individual packets of medications, such as cold, allergy and headache medicine.

9. Assemble a mini sewing kit by wrapping different threads around a small piece of chipboard and sticking needles and safety pins into a swatch of fabric.

10. Pack the items in the tin and place a label on the lid.

11. Pack all the items in the zipper pouch and attach a tag to the zipper that says, "Hurry home!"

I have found myself traveling quite a bit lately, and I enjoy little reminders of home. So when Colton, my five-and-a-half year old, drew this little airplane complete with a pilot in the cockpit, I instantly knew it would look adorable on *travel kit* labels. Colton was eager to help write the name of the contents and pour the products in bottles. I can't wait to watch him give away his creations!

When I saw this cute little *tote* at a craft store, it seemed just the right size for a child to carry. I used it to create a gift set that would be easy to duplicate and could keep kids entertained. My kids love any reason to use the sewing machine, and two straight-stitched seams is all it takes to make the pockets for the pencils. Handwritten titles add charm to this gift.

GAME BAG

1. Buy a pre-made canvas tote. Have a child help you stitch two seams down each side to hold the pencils.

2. Have the child write a title on a piece of canvas. Mask off the handwriting and paint around the edge. Cut with pinking sheers.

3. Use a fabric adhesive or buttons to secure the canvas title to the bag.

4. Decorate pencils by gluing a small piece of patterned paper around the end. Use ribbon to tie on a tag that designates player one and player two.

5. Create artwork for the notepads on a computer or draw simple games for children to play. Have a child write the name of the game on the top of the artwork. Note: Having notepads made is simple. Have the artwork photocopied at a copy store. Have them cut the paper to notepad size and ask them to create notepads by gumming and padding the games. Having the notepads made is very inexpensive and can be done in a day.

Buttons: Making Memories
Jewelry tags: Avery
Paint: Delta
Paper: Making Memories
Pinking sheers: Fiskars
Ribbon: Offray
Other: Canvas, canvas bag and pencils

GAMES TO GO | By Robin Johnson

SEED-COVERED BIRDHOUSE | By Erin Terrell

My mom has always been an avid crafter, and I remember she shared that love with me when I was young. We had so much fun with our creations, and I proudly showed off each of my handmade projects. The messiest crafts were always my favorites! That's why this birdhouse is so much fun for kids. Daisy and I took our *birdhouse* outside and set it on a sheet of newspaper while we were painting on the birdseed, then we rinsed off with the hose when we were finished. Daisy loved it and already wants to know when we can make another one!

BIRDHOUSE

1. Paint the birdhouse with primer so it can be used outdoors.

2. Mix equal parts of Elmer's Glue and water in a container, then mix in the birdseed. Erin warns that you'll have a sticky, gooey mess!

3. Use an old paintbrush to paint one coat of birdseed all over the birdhouse. Allow to dry for 24 hours.

4. Paint another coat of birdseed on the birdhouse and allow to dry.

5. Paint any exposed edges of the birdhouse with paint.

Birdseed: Kaytee Supreme
Gel paint: Golden
Glue: Elmer's
Other: Birdhouse

When making gifts with kids, let them be creative. Encourage them to pick their own colors of ribbon and embellishments. If it doesn't match, it's okay—that's part of the charm. These **bookmarks** make a much-appreciated gift for teachers and other adults, as well as for your child's young friends. Give them alone or tucked in a favorite book.

FLOWER WITH GREEN RIBBON BOOKMARK

1. Cut a piece of ribbon so when folded in half it will be long enough for a bookmark.

2. Emboss an Eyelet Charm with two or three coats of white embossing enamel.

3. Tie a decorative thread through a button. Attach to the embossed flower with an adhesive dot.

4. Thread ribbon through the hole of the Eyelet Charm and fasten with a snap.

5. Stitch a button to the bottom of each ribbon.

BUTTON ON PINK RIBBON BOOKMARK

1. Cut a piece of ribbon so when folded in half it will be long enough for a bookmark.

2. Stitch the buttons near the top with Scrapbook Stitches.

3. Add decorative snaps to the ends.

FRAMED DRAWING BOOKMARK

1. Have a child draw a picture in the frame.

2. Cut a piece of ribbon so when folded in half it will be long enough for a bookmark.

3. Thread ribbon through the frame and secure with a snap.

4. Crimp a scrap of a Metal Sheet over the ends of the ribbon. You may need to use a double-sided adhesive to make sure the metal remains in place.

Buttons, eyelet charm, metal sheet, scrapbook stitches and snaps: Making Memories
Colored pencils: Prismacolor
Embossing enamel: Ultra Thick Embossing Enamel, Suze Weinberg
Embossing ink: Ranger Industries
Frame: Nunn Designs
Ribbon: May Arts

BOOKMARKS | By Julie Turner

FRAME FOR DRAWINGS | By Jennifer Jensen

FRAME

1. Have your child draw and color a picture of himself with the loved one to whom you're giving the frame.

2. Have him write or dictate a message for the recipient.

3. Trace his handprint and include his age or the date.

4. Find or take a photograph with your child and the person to whom you're giving the frame.

5. Find a picture frame with four slots in which to put the above items.

6. Hang Eyelet Charms from fiber and add Eyelet Letters to the frame.

Alphabet charms, charmed photo corners, defined sticker, eyelet charms, eyelet letters and funky with fiber: Making Memories
Frame: Decorel
Paper: Making Memories

I love kids' handwriting and the way they write stories. I wanted to incorporate this in a special way for the kids' grammy. I wanted my son to write some of the reasons why he thinks grammy is so special to him, then draw a picture that shows how he views himself and his grammy together. I know this would be a great gift for any child to give to a loved one.

By using original ways of presenting your gifts, you can make the wrapping as much of a gift as what's inside. This chapter will have you wrapping differently this holiday season as you learn artistic ways to wrap money and gift cards, decorate a plain gift box or create your own gift bag. The recipient will know how much you care even before opening the package!

CHECKBOOK BOX | By Jennifer Jensen
GIFT CARD TIN BOX | By Stephanie McAtee

I like unique *packaging*. I want the recipient to get that "wow" factor and to love the packaging as much as the gift itself! For these projects, use miscellaneous boxes and tins found around the home. Try painting, decoupaging or covering boxes with fabric. The checkbook box and the Altoid tin are the perfect size to hold a gift card or small gift.

CHECKBOOK BOX

1. Remove the lid from a checkbook box—you'll only be using the bottom of the box for this project.

2. Cover the box with decorative paper.

3. Cut a piece of mat board to go around the bottom, back side and top of the box. Score the mat board so it can wrap around the box like a book cover.

4. Glue the bottom and back side of the box to the mat board, letting the top flap over. Underneath, between the mat and the bottom of the box, remember to insert ribbon, fiber or string to tie the box closed.

5. Decorate the mat board as desired.

6. To create the closure on the top of the box, glue two buttons together—one on top of the other—and tie the string from the bottom around to secure.

Charmed frame and eyelet letters:
Making Memories
Embossing enamel: Ultra Thick Embossing
Enamel, Suze Weinberg
Fibers: On the Surface
Rubber stamp: JudiKins
Other: Buttons, foam board, jute, mat board
and tassel

TIN BOX

1. Paint an Altoid tin with acrylic paint.

2. Print a word on twill tape by affixing the tape to a sheet of paper with double-stick tape and running it through your printer.

3. Decoupage assorted ephemera to the tin lid.

4. Decoupage tissue paper and a number on a domino.

5. Create a magnet with the domino and angel wings. Stick to the top of the tin.

6. Decorate a cardstock pouch in which to slide the actual gift card.

#2: FoofaLa
Computer font: Willing Race, downloaded
from the Internet
Paint: Delta
Paper: Anna Griffin
Photo corner: Kolo
Sticker: Nostalgiques, EK Success
Other: Altoid tin, angel wings, domino,
label maker, magnet strip, old family photo,
old Lotto card, tissue paper and twill tape

CHALKBOARD TAGS | BY HEIDI SWAPP

TAGS

1. Prime both sides of a wooden tag and allow to dry.

2. Spray chalkboard paint evenly on both sides of the tag. Allow to dry, then apply a second coat.

3. Write on the tags with chalk.

4. Tie the tag onto a wrapped package.

---

*Bead chain, charms and twistel: Making Memories
Other: Chalk, chalkboard spray paint, jute,
kraft-colored wrapping paper, primer, twine
and wooden tags*

I am not the type of person who carefully removes beautiful wrapping paper so it can be tucked in a drawer and reused. What is the fun in that? But these chalkboard *tags* are something I can see myself putting back into circulation. In order to reuse them, wipe the name off with a dry cloth, then wipe it again with a damp cloth and dry. It will come totally clean!

It's fun to think of different ways to

designate which gift

or stocking belongs to whom. Instead of a

tag on a gift or having names on a stocking,

you can use photos and initials. I loved using

the metal frames because I could paint them

to make them match perfectly. I can't wait to

hang the stockings above our fireplace on an

old coat hook.

STOCKINGS

1. Cut a stocking pattern from heavyweight paper. Pin to your fabric. Remember to cut a front and back piece.

2. Make a cuff for the top of each stocking and sew stocking together.

3. Trim with buttons, patches, ribbon and fabric-covered buttons. Use fray check on the ends of the ribbon.

4. Paint an Eyelet Letter with a primer. Once dry, paint the letter to match the stocking. Allow to dry, then heat emboss with clear embossing enamel. Hang the letter from the fabric-covered button with wire.

5. Paint the Charmed Frames with a primer. Allow to dry. Add a photo behind the frame and set an eyelet in the top corner of the photo.

6. Heat emboss the frame with clear embossing enamel. Rhonda allowed some of the enamel to get on the edges of her photo.

7. String ribbon through the eyelet and hang from the fabric-covered button.

Button-covering kit: Dritz
Buttons, charmed frames, eyelet letters,
eyelets and wire: Making Memories
Embossing enamel: Ultra Thick Embossing
Enamel, Suze Weinberg
Paint: Delta
Primer: Kilz
Other: Fabric, fray check and ribbon

VINTAGE-INSPIRED CHRISTMAS STOCKINGS | By Rhonda Solomon

DECOUPAGED GIFT BOX | By Jennifer Jensen

GIFT BOX

1. Choose the box you would like to decoupage and gather enough coordinating fabrics to cover the lid.

2. Tear or cut the fabrics into various shapes.

3. Glue fabric onto box, layering the pieces as you go.

4. Apply a decoupage medium over the top and let dry.

5. Tie a tulle ribbon around the entire box.

Adhesive: Mod Podge, Plaid
Tag: Avery
Walnut ink: Postmodern Design
Other: Box, fabric, ribbon, rick rack and tulle

I thought this project would be something unique and easy and could be reused another year. I used a gift *box* I already had and simply decorated the lid. I also used tulle to tie the bow on this box. I love using tulle to wrap my presents. Any way you tie them, you end up with a fast, fluffy and fabulous bow! The tag on this gift represents something that happens in our family every year on Christmas day...When the kids wake up on Christmas morning, they know exactly which gifts came from Santa and who they are for, simply by the initial on the tag. Santa must be pretty crafty!

Wrapping has always been an important part of

giving to me. I like giving gifts in a reusable gift

container. It's really two

gifts in one! Whether you start with a placemat

or a Chinese take-out box, there is a lot of

versatility with these concepts. The best part

is that both ideas are simple and affordable.

TAKE-OUT CONTAINER

1. Take apart a Chinese take-out container and trace the outline onto pearl-colored paper.

2. Score the folds and glue the paper to the outside of the box.

3. Fold the box back into shape.

4. String a button through the top hanger of each tassel. Attach the tassels and ribbon handle before hot gluing the sides of the container.

5. Add Metal Words to the sides of the container.

Buttons: Dress It Up
Metal words: Making Memories
Paper: Provo Craft
Tassels: Wrights
Other: Chinese take-out container and ribbon

PLACEMAT BAG

1. Fold the bottom of a placemat up about 2" from the top. Machine stitch a seam on each side.

2. To make the snowflake "fossil" buttons, pour embossing powder in metal frames, then melt with a heat gun. Press a snowflake stamp into the warm powder. When cool, rub with metallic rub-ons.

3. Drill small holes in cooled "fossils," then stitch onto bag, putting a smaller button underneath so they are slightly raised.

4. Wind wire around the fossils to close.

5. Attach snowflake charm and tag to the square fossil.

Alphabet stamps: PSX Design
Charmed snowflake, eyelet and wire: Making Memories
Embossing enamel: Ultra Thick Embossing Enamel, Suze Weinberg
Metallic rub-ons: Craf-T Products
Snowflake rubber stamp: Stampin' Up!
Other: Gold frames and placemat

PLACEMAT GIFT BAG | By Rhonda Solomon
CHINESE TAKE-OUT | By Kris Stanger

MONEY BOOK | By Julie Turner
DRAWSTRING BAG | By Jennifer Jensen
BELIEVE GIFT BAG | By Emily Waters

Fabric *bags* are quick and easy to make. Two straight-stitched lines and it's done!

You can make them as big or as small as you like. Threading ribbon through eyelets at the top

of the bag is an easy way to make it drawstring. This is a great way to wrap odd-shaped gifts.

MONEY BOOK

1. Make a mini book with Charmed Frame covers to hold a "money gift."

2. To connect the left sides of the frames, attach ribbon to the back of the frame with an adhesive dot. Run the ribbon through the opening of the frame, through a Ribbon Charm and through the opening of the other frame, attaching it to the back with an adhesive dot.

3. Fold two bills just smaller than the Charmed Frames. Julie used one dollar bills on the covers—the faces on other bills are too big.

4. Adhere one bill to each frame with adhesive dots, so Washington's face is framed.

5. Create a closure for the right side following the same steps used to create the left-side closure.

6. Slide additional folded bills down between the frames.

Charmed frames and ribbon charms:
Making Memories
Ribbon: May Arts
Other: Money

BELIEVE BAG

1. Cut a long rectangle from fabric.

2. Fold the bottom part up, leaving enough for a top flap. Stitch along two sides and the top flap to create a bag.

3. Attach Eyelet Shapes and string for the closure.

4. Add an image to the bag with a large foam stamp and paint.

5. Apply a Simply Stated rub-on to the front.

Eyelet shapes and simply stated rub-ons:
Making Memories
Other: Fabric, foam stamp, string and tag

DRAWSTRING BAG

1. Cut a rectangle from fabric. Make the rectangle twice as long as you want your bag. Fold in half—wrong sides together—then sew a straight stitch along each side.

2. Turn right side out. Fold down a cuff. (You could make the bag a little longer by not folding a cuff.)

3. Set an eyelet approximately every 1" around the top of the bag or cuff.

4. Weave ribbon in and out of the eyelets, then tie in a bow.

Eyelets and simply stated rub-ons:
Making Memories
Other: Fabric and ribbon

Advent calendars are the perfect way to mark the days until Christmas, adding extra excitement and anticipation to the season. Give your family something to remember and look forward to each day with a story, tradition or favorite seasonal photo. Watch the suspense build as you count down to #1, and herald in the holiday season with a handmade advent calendar!

PHOTO FLIP ADVENT CALENDAR | By Jennifer Jensen

I decided to write a poem to begin the advent

calendar. In the poem, I

wrote about what Christmas means to me and the

thoughts and feelings of the season. I decided

each page would be something that is a symbol of

Christmas for our family. I thought that this

would be a fun way to count down to Christmas.

I also incorporated photos from past holidays on

each page.

FLIP CALENDAR
1. Decorate the front of a photo
flip frame.
2. Decorate each page with photos,
embellishments and other items that
represent your family's favorite
Christmas memories.
3. Proceed to count down the days until
Christmas, using Eyelet Numbers on each
page until reaching the number one.

"25 days" tag: Paperbilities
Black ribbon: Bucilla
Embossing enamel: Ultra Thick Embossing
Enamel, Suze Weinberg
Embossing powder: Stampin' Up!
Eyelet numbers, magnetic date stamp, metal
frames and shaped clips: Making Memories
Paper: Making Memories and The Paper Company
Photo flip frame: Furio Home
Wood corner: Walnut Hollow
Other: Beads, bell, buttons, red ribbon and
vintage lace

ADVENT CALENDAR | By Stephanie McAtee

CALENDAR

1. Decoupage the magazine cover onto galvanized steel.

2. Randomly paint around the edges of the steel.

3. Cut thin strips of cardstock to divide the days of the calendar and make labels for the days of the week.

4. Create numbers from various items: Alphabet Charms, dominos, rubber stamps, game cards, etc.

5. Glue magnet strips to the backs of Christmas-themed items and add to the steel.

6. Decoupage small tins and leave notes inside for that day's surprise.

Adhesive: Mod Podge, Plaid
Alphabet charms, eyelet alphabet, simply stated rub-on and snap: Making Memories
Paint: Delta
Tags: Avery
Other: Altoid tin, assorted ephemera, cover from The Saturday Evening Post, found objects, galvanized steel and wire

I wanted my advent calendar to represent my visuals of Christmas: fun, creative, traditions and trend. I want to be able to re-create the advent calendar each year—to add to, take away from or change. That is where I got the idea to use the magnetized base and to attach mini *magnets* on the backs of the small decoupaged tins, numbers, small Santa photos, etc. I was going for a synergy of elements to create a fun advent calendar, visually and traditionally.

During the holiday season when days get hectic,

it's so easy to get caught up in our "to do" lists

and lose sight of the real reason we're so busy.

I love taking a few moments each evening to

regain my focus, *teach* my children

and enjoy family time together. This advent book

is a perfect way to do just that. For each day there

is a different story to read. I've also created an

ornament for each story that we place on the tree.

ADVENT BOOK

1. Adhere red patterned paper to the album cover with Mod Podge. Leave a 1" border around the outside.

2. Tear sheet music to fit in the lower right corner and shade with brown and black ink. Adhere to red paper with Mod Podge.

3. Cut a tag shape from a Defined sticker. Ink the edges with brown and black ink. Cut another tag from peach-colored vellum and ink the edges.

4. Attach the vellum tag over the definition tag with adhesive dots. Set an eyelet on the tag.

5. Trim eyelets from the Eyelet Letters, glue the Metal Word onto the tag and stamp "'til" in the middle with Staz-On ink.

6. Adhere holly die cuts to cover.

7. Paint the entire front cover with Mod Podge. Allow to dry.

8. Attach a tassel to the tag and adhere to the cover.

9. Glue braided trim around the border.

10. Collect 24 of your favorite Christmas stories. For the 24th, the Lewis family uses the account of Jesus' birth from the New Testament.

11. Create or find simple ornaments to represent each story, and each night when a story is read, hang the corresponding ornament on your Christmas tree.

Adhesive: *Mod Podge, Plaid*
Alphabet stamps: *PSX Design*
Defined sticker, eyelet, eyelet letters, metal word and star page pebble: *Making Memories*
Die cuts: *K & Company*
Paper: *Frances Meyer*
Photo album: *Pioneer*
Stamping ink: *StazOn, Tsukineko; Clearsnap*
Tassel: *Hirschberg Schutz & Co.*
Other: *Black braid, sheet music and vellum*

24 DAYS 'TIL CHRISTMAS ADVENT BOOK | By Sharon Lewis

TRADITION MINI BOOK | By Heidi Swapp

From the time I was little, one of my favorite things about the Christmas season has been the advent calendar. I find that my life gets so crazy during the holidays that I forget all the little things that meant so much to me as a child. Each page in this book suggests something to do *to* celebrate the season, such as trimming the tree, writing a letter to Santa or lining the yard with luminaries. The holiday tradition "assignments" are tucked here and there on the pages of the book. I hope it will be a lifelong holiday tradition.

MINI BOOK

1. Paint the album cover red.

2. Tie a tatted snowflake and ribbon to a hook. Glue to the cover.

3. Embellish the rest of the cover with Metal Words, an Eyelet Phrase and an Eyelet Charm set with a snap.

4. Coat the completed cover with Mod Podge.

5. Determine the traditions or activities you want to include. Be sure your book can accommodate 25 days.

6. Label each page with "day one," "day two," "day three," etc.

7. Create a pocket or envelope for each page and embellish as desired.

8. For example, on day four, the Swapps have a tradition of writing letters to Santa, then putting them in their shoes for St. Nicholas on Dec. 5th.

9. To create the page, mount cardstock on album page.

10. Zigzag stitch along the flap of an envelope, catching a small ribbon tab in the stitch. Adhere the envelope to the page.

11. Embellish with Charmed Photo Corners, a vintage stamp and a Simply Stated rub-on.

12. Write the assignment on a card and tuck inside the envelope. Secure the flap with a small piece of Velcro.

13. For the December 14th page, decoupage tissue paper to album page and allow to dry.

14. Cut an envelope in half, age with chalks, then adhere to page.

15. Adhere a Metal Word to a star shape cut from a Metal Sheet. Paint, then decoupage over the star.

16. Punch two holes in the star and fashion a wire hanger.

17. Attach to a piece of brown cardstock that has been cut to fit in the envelope.

18. Embellish the brown cardstock with an Eyelet Phrase, a washer and calendar sticker.

19. Write that day's assignment on the insert and tuck into the envelope.

20. Cut a Defined sticker into little words and place on page.

21. Embellish the rest of the page with ribbon and photo corners.

Other page ideas include: letters to Santa, decorating the home, listening to favorite Christmas music and sorting through toys to donate to charity.

Adhesive: *Mod Podge, Plaid*
Album: *7 Gypsies*
Charmed photo corners, defined sticker, eyelet charm, eyelet phrases, magnetic date stamp, metal sheet, metal words, simply stated rub-on, snaps and wire:
Making Memories
Envelopes: *Paper Source*
Mini calendar: *Nostalgiques, EK Success*
Paint: *Plaid*
Paper: *Making Memories*
Ribbon: *May Arts and Offray*
Tatted snowflake: *Becky Criddle*
Other: *Hook, photo corners, postage stamp, tissue paper, Velcro and washer*

After the first Christmas card was made in the 1840s, the idea of sending holiday greetings caught on. Now millions are exchanged every year. Hand-making cards takes time and creativity, but the joy of creating them and the delight of receiving one is priceless. Whether you fashion a poinsettia for the front, include a family photo or add a touching sentiment, follow the lead of those who originated the tradition and create your own miniature works of art.

NOEL | By Sharon Lewis
MANGER CARD | By Kris Stanger

It is so fun to get creative photos of your children, especially during the holidays! I shot this manger scene for a good friend of mine to use in her Christmas *cards*. It was fairly simple. There wasn't any major sewing involved; the kids just wore pieces of fabric and swaddling. I shot it in black and white film and had it developed in sepia tone.

NOEL CARD

1. Fold a piece of 12"x 6" cardstock in half to form a card. Ink the edges to age.

2. Cut a piece of patterned paper to a 5 ¾" square. Rubber stamp accents on the patterned paper. Adhere to the front of the card with Mod Podge.

3. Cut a poinsettia from patterned paper. Decoupage to the front of the card with Mod Podge. Glue beads to the center of the flower using Diamond Glaze.

4. Cut Wooden Tile stickers and ink the edges. Affix to a rectangular piece of cardstock. Decoupage to the card, and frame with a tag Eyelet Charm.

5. Add a decorative corner made from pinked patterned paper.

Adhesives: Diamond Glaze, JudiKins;
Mod Podge, Plaid
Beads: Westrim
Eyelet charm, snaps and wooden tile stickers:
Making Memories
Foam stamps: Duncan
Paper: 7 Gypsies, Daisy D's, Karen Foster
Design and Magenta
Stamping ink: Clearsnap

MANGER CARD

1. Create a card from cardstock.

2. Cut a small strip of paper to create a closure. Glue half of the closure to the back of the card. Attach Velcro to the front of the card and to the other half of the closure strip.

3. Chalk around the edges of the card.

4. Attach photo and embellishments, then adhere cardstock to the inside of the card for your message.

5. Tie jute around the fold of the card and hang the "Peace on Earth" tag.

Alphabet stamps: PSX Design
Charmed photo corners and eyelet shape:
Making Memories
Paper: Making Memories
Stamping inks: Ranger Industries and
Stampin' Up!
Textured paper: Provo Craft
Other: Chalk, jute and Velcro

ALTERED-BOOK CARD HOLDER | By Erin Trimble

BOOK

1. Cover an old book as desired with lightweight paper. Be sure to smooth out all wrinkles and miter the corners to create a clean cover. The embossed paper around the spine of the book started off yellow. Erin added purple metallic rub-ons, making it coordinate better with the purple papers.

2. Embellish the front with layered paper photo corners and a Charmed Sled. Add a frame with a title written inside.

3. Alter the inside pages of the book to hold the Christmas cards you receive from friends and family.

4. To make the pictured pocket, paint a left-hand page with Lumiere. Cover the bottom third of the opposite page with patterned paper. When dry, turn the page, then paint the left-hand page with Lumiere and cover the top two-thirds of the opposite page with patterned paper. When dry, turn back to the first two altered pages. Carefully tear the right-hand page near the spine, two-thirds of the way down. Fold the torn page down three or four times to make a cuff. Glue the edge of the bottom and right-hand side of the pocket to the back page. Secure the cuff with a Shaped Clip.

Charmed sled and shaped clip: Making Memories
Metallic rub-ons: Craf-T Products
Paint: Lumiere, Jacquard Products
Paper: Making Memories and K & Company
Silver frame: Nunn Designs
Other: Embossed paper and heart charm

After taking an altered-book class with my mom, I thought an altered book would be a clever way to showcase the Christmas cards my husband and I receive each year. You can make the *book* ahead of time, altering the inside pages to create pockets. When you receive a card, tuck it in one of the pockets. Make a new book for each year and get them out for a festive decoration and to bring back fond memories.

Family photos can be an opportunity to enhance Christmas greetings. Whether it's Santa hats that bring out the *ho, ho, ho* or faces that emulate the joy of Christmas, family photos send a cheerful Christmas message. The concept of using letters in your photos can be adapted, depending on how many family members you have ("peace" for 5 family members, "noel" for 4, etc.). For larger families, take one family shot with each member holding a letter.

HO HO HO CARD

1. Cut three strips of red paper and cut a window out of each one. Instead of using paper, you could use also cut strips of burlap, corrugated cardboard or felt.

2. Glue a hinge to the back of each strip, then glue a strip of red cardstock to the back to create a sturdier panel. Stitch around the outside edges of the outer two panels.

3. Spray paint the letters and seal, then glue onto the accordion card.

4. Set an eyelet at the bottom of the first panel. String a bell, a painted metal-rimmed tag, an Eyelet Charm and a fabric scrap on a length of bead chain.

Adhesive: Metal Glue, Making Memories
Alphabet stamps: PSX Design
Bead chain, eyelet, eyelet charm, eyelet letters, hinges and metal-rimmed tag: Making Memories
Paint: Delta
Spray paint: Krylon
Other: Bell, burlap, corrugated paper, ribbon and velveteen paper

WISHING YOU JOY CARD

1. Cut a card from red paper. Leave room for a 1" flap along the bottom that will fold up.

2. Do a photo shoot using letters to spell out a holiday message. Print wallet-sized photos.

3. Cut and collage scraps of red patterned paper to create a background.

4. Mount the photos on green cardstock, leaving an allowance at the top for a bow.

5. Create the bows by unwinding strips of Twistel and running it through Ribbon Charms. Adhere to the card with adhesive dots.

6. Stamp your message, then frame it in a metal frame. Hang the frame from a knotted strip of Twistel.

7. Run red gingham ribbon through more Ribbon Charms, then adhere to the flap at the bottom. Cut small pieces of Velcro to hold the flap shut. The flap folds out so the card can open.

8. Write "joy" repeatedly along the bottom flap.

Jump ring, ribbon charms and Twistel: Making Memories
Metal frame: Scrapworks
Paper: Making Memories and Paper Fever
Pen: EK Success
Stamping ink: Memories
Other: Alphabet stamps, ribbon and Velcro

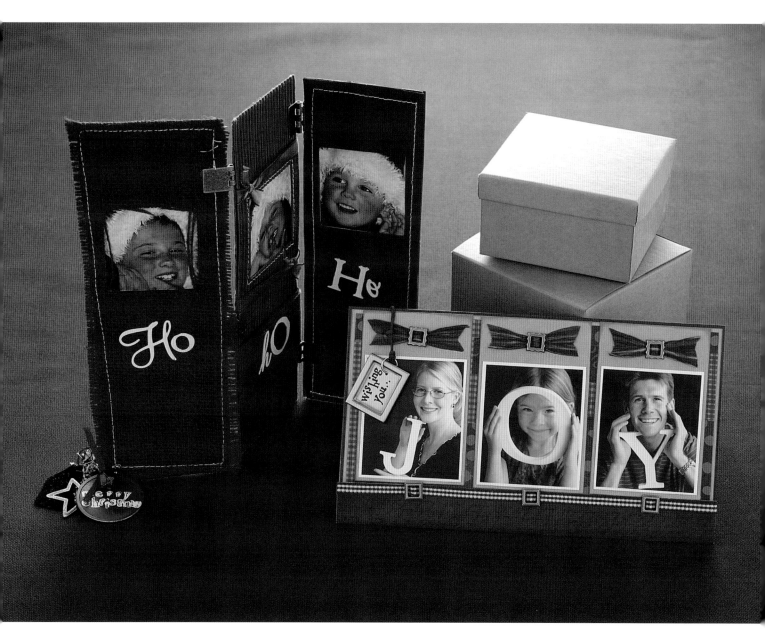

HO HO HO | By Jennifer Jensen
WISHING YOU JOY | By Erin Terrell

Creating Christmas cards will bring out your holiday spirit more than anything else! Photographs of children, whether siblings or cousins, evoke the *warmth* and hope of the Christmas season.

BETTER NOT POUT... CARD

1. Affix a photo to patterned paper and add coordinating photo corners.

2. Layer various sizes of printed and plain papers. Tear some of the paper and ink some of the edges to age. Print or rubber stamp your message on plain paper.

3. Put a transparency over the top and machine stitch the papers together on the left-hand side.

4. Print a message on twill tape by affixing the tape to a sheet of paper with double-stick tape and running it through your printer.

5. Secure the printed twill tape to the transparency with eyelets.

6. For a finishing touch, heat emboss a tree Eyelet Charm and add ribbon through the hole. Hang from the card with a jump ring and bead chain.

Alphabet stamps, bead chain, eyelet charm, eyelets and jump ring: Making Memories
Computer font: Willing Race, downloaded from the Internet
Embossing enamel: Ultra Thick Embossing Enamel, Suze Weinberg
Paper: Anna Griffin and Bazzill Basics
Photo corners: Kolo
Stamping ink: Clearsnap
Other: Old book paper, ribbon, transparency and twill tape

TURNER CARD

CARD

1. Cut a paper template the size of the card. Because the card will have some bulk, cut it slightly smaller so it fits easily into the envelope.

2. Roll out the paper clay just as you would roll out a pie crust. Lay the template onto the clay and cut out with a knife.

3. Stamp the date into the soft clay. If you don't like the result, roll up the clay and try again. If the clay gets dry, add a small amount of water.

4. Allow to dry for 24 hours.

ENVELOPE

1. Cut a piece of natural-colored cotton canvas large enough to create an envelope.

2. Paint one side with white gesso.

3. When dry, cut an envelope using a die cut machine or template. Fold into shape.

4. Attach eyelets for the tie, then tape the seams together using double-sided photo tape. Julie also suggests hand stitching the envelope together.

5. Tie the flap closed with a piece of fiber. If you are sending the card through the mail, secure the flap with double-sided tape.

6. Hand address the envelopes directly on the gessoed canvas, run it through a computer (before folding the canvas together) or tape or sew labels onto the envelope.

Computer font: Sylfaen
Eyelets, magnetic date stamp and safety pin: Making Memories
Gesso: Liquitex
Nailhead: 7 Gypsies
Paper clay: Creative Paperclay
Other: Canvas, fiber and rubber bands

BETTER NOT POUT... | By Heidi Swapp
THE TURNERS | By Julie Turner

HOLIDAY ELEMENT | By Stephanie McAtee
BELIEVE TAG CARD | By Emily Waters

Looking to do something different than just the usual Christmas card that everybody makes? Create a *tag* book and make a tag about each family member using embellishments and words that best describe each person. Include journaling to tell what each child has been up to that year. Another unique concept is to use past photos on current Christmas cards. Relive the memories as you embellish them.

ELEMENT CARD

1. Cut off two sides of a string and button envelope so it will completely open.

2. Remove the button closures from the envelope.

3. Add a strip of book-binding tape to the top flap.

4. Replace the button closures with Washer Words and secure with eyelets.

5. Rubber stamp the date on a black and white photo and affix to the layout with photo corners.

6. Place alphabet stickers inside button covers and place at the top of the photo.

7. Fold a bingo card over one side of the card. Adhere in place.

8. Embellish the rest of the envelope with alphabet stamps and a word made with a label maker.

9. Brush acrylic paint on various places on the card.

Alphabet stickers: Nostalgiques, EK Success
Button covers: FoofaLa
Eyelets, magnetic alphabet stamp, magnetic date stamp and washer words: Making Memories
Paint: Delta
Photo corners: Kolo
String and button envelope:
www.twopeasinabucket.com
Other: Bingo card, book-binding tape and label maker

TAG CARD

1. Cut a front and back cover from lightweight cardboard. Brush on walnut ink to give the tags an aged look.

2. Attach a Defined sticker with staples, and machine stitch a square of red fabric to the front.

3. Print out a large initial (to represent last name), then trace it onto black cardstock and cut out.

4. Paint cream paint around the letter to give it a shabby look. Adhere the letter to the fabric square.

5. Create a reinforced hole at the top of the tag using a circle punch and a pewter eyelet.

6. Type up paragraphs about each child and print them on desired paper. Cut out in a tag shape. Brush on walnut ink to age.

7. Adhere a photo and embellishments as desired.

8. When all the tags are complete, attach the tags with bead chain.

9. Attach a small tag onto the bead chain using ribbon to spell out the family's last name.

Bead chain, defined stickers, eyelets, ribbon, snap and staples: Making Memories
Paint: Delta
Paper: Bazzill Basics
Other: Fabric and tag

CHRISTMAS TREE CARD | By Robin Johnson
COLLAGE CHRISTMAS CARD | By Erin Trimble

Creating Christmas cards can work with anyone's time schedule. From the simple to the complex, your homemade cards will be appreciated. The tree is a clean, timeless design with just a touch of fiber to accent. The *collage* card contains various sizes and types of papers, from tags to envelopes to transparencies. Have fun collecting and arranging your pages to create this unique card.

TREE CARD

1. Cut a piece of paper to 7½"x 8½". Fold the paper in half.

2. Cut a long triangle from green paper. Divide into thirds and fold at the marks.

3. Tape one end of the fiber to the back side and wrap around the tree. Tape the other end to the back of the tree to secure.

4. Tear a piece of patterned paper and glue to the front of the card. Place tree on top.

5. Cut tree trunk from corrugated cardboard. Glue under the tree.

6. To alter the metal pieces, brush paint into the grooves and wipe off the excess with a wet wipe. Adhere to cardstock.

Charmed star, eyelet words and funky with fiber: Making Memories
Corrugated cardboard: DMD Industries
Paper: Making Memories and 7 Gypsies

COLLAGE CARD

1. Cut two pieces of white cardstock to form the covers of the card.

2. Wet and crinkle the paper, then smooth it out. Dip in walnut ink to age.

3. Embellish the front cover by mixing paper photo corners, Charmed Photo Corners and rubber stamps. Hang an Eyelet Charm from a tinker pin.

4. Gather various sizes of papers, envelopes and ephemera for the inside pages. Erin used a tag, glassine envelope, Defined sticker and photo just to name a few.

5. Arrange the papers so they are uneven and varied in their placement between the two covers.

6. Hand stitch or machine stitch a binding on the left side. Score a fold just to the right of the binding so the card is easier to open.

Alphabet stamps: PSX Design
Charmed photo corner, defined sticker and eyelet charm: Making Memories
Paper: Making Memories
Rubber stamp: Hampton Art Stamps
Tag: Avery
Tinker pin: 7 Gypsies
Walnut ink: Postmodern Design
Other: Kraft bag, screen, vellum envelope and waxed linen

Instead of traditional red and green, use a black background to create a *classic*, timeless feel. Try using black for the photo background, for the mat or for the card itself.

On the "Joy" card, you can tuck photos, newsletters, Christmas stories or an invitation behind the ribbon.

MONTGOMERY CARD

1. Adhere printed paper to chipboard with spray adhesive.

2. Miter the corners and fold the edges around to the back of the chipboard.

3. Cut an opening for your photo with an X-Acto knife.

4. Cut a square of velvet and trace the opening of your photo mat with a white colored pencil.

5. Cut an X shape within the outline of the opening.

6. Place the fabric over the covered chipboard and fold the flaps behind the opening, completely covering the inside edges of the chipboard.

7. Secure the fabric to the frame by machine stitching around the opening.

8. String charms on an elastic and attach to the front of the card, slightly over the photo.

9. Add a tag on the right side with a metal clamp.

10. Print your family newsletter on coordinating paper and adhere to the back of the frame.

Elastic: Darice
Eyelets, ornament charms and ribbon:
Making Memories
Jewelry tag: American Tag
Paper: Penny Black
Other: Metal clamp, split rings, spring coils
and velvet

JOY CARD

1. Cut a strip of black cardstock to fit desired envelope.

2. Secure a piece of red gingham ribbon across the strip with Eyelet Alphabet letters. Wrap the edges of the ribbon around to the back.

3. Print your family newsletter onto a folding tag and embellish.

4. Tuck the newsletter and a photo behind the ribbon.

Eyelet, eyelet alphabet and page pebble:
Making Memories
Gingham ribbon: Garden Gate Designs
Paper: Making Memories and 7 Gypsies
Other: Green ribbon and rick rack

MONTGOMERY'S 2001 | By Lynne Montgomery

JOY | By Erin Trimble

MERRY CHRISTMAS FRINGE CARD | By Rhonda Solomon

PEACE ON EARTH | By Erin Trimble

Making Christmas cards is a perfect opportunity to spend time as a family and to reinforce family beliefs. Listen to Christmas music as you involve your children in the fun and let them play Santa's elves as they deliver the cards. The *peace on earth* card was designed with a rustic, old-fashioned look that is reminiscent of the simplicity of Christ's birth.

CHRISTMAS FRINGE CARD

1. Fold an 8½" x 11" piece of cardstock in half to create a card.

2. Color block the card with cardstock and printed paper. Allow 1" to hang off the card to make fringe.

3. For the star tree, stamp image onto light mustard cardstock and heat emboss with copper powder. Use brown ribbon for the trunk.

4. Create holly leaves, berries and branches with cardstock.

5. Paint a snowflake Eyelet Charm with acrylic paint, pour embossing powder over the top and heat emboss.

6. Stamp "merry" using various alphabet stamps and ink colors. Cut out, then ink the edges. Glue pieces of rick rack above and below the word.

7. Create the mini envelope with cardstock and mini eyelets, using tweezers to hold the small pieces.

8. Rubber stamp a snowflake on a tag Eyelet Charm. Put a safety pin through each hole and attach to card with adhesive dots.

9. Glue Alphabet Charms to the card and put a drop of Diamond Glaze on top.

10. Use adhesive dots to affix buttons to the card.

11. Stitch around the outside edges of the card.

12. Cut into outside edges to create fringe.

13. Dry brush over the card with a large stippling brush and black acrylic paint.

Adhesive: Diamond Glaze, JudiKins
Alphabet charms, eyelet charm, eyelets
and safety pins: Making Memories
Rubber stamps: Hero Arts, PSX Design and
Stampin' Up!
Stamping ink: Tsukineko
Other: Paint and rick rack

PEACE ON EARTH CARD

1. Create a card from cardboard. Because of the card's bulk, make sure it'll fit inside your envelope before embellishing.

2. Paint a background for the white lettering with acrylic paint. Allow to dry, then apply a Simply Stated rub-on.

3. Back the Charmed Frame and star with a frayed fabric scrap.

4. Print a sentiment onto text-weight paper and cut it just smaller than the cardboard card. Fold in half.

5. Bind the text-weight paper to the cardboard card with waxed linen. Run beads through the binding for added interest.

Charmed frame, charmed star and
simply stated rub-on: Making Memories
Paint: Delta
Other: Beads, cardboard, fabric and
waxed linen

When the decorations are put away and all the goodies have been gobbled down, the holiday season can still be remembered through photos and fond memories. You can capture what is unique and special about that year's Christmas events with a scrapbook page. Cherish those moments for years to come by using the following ideas to showcase your family's holiday memories in a creative and pleasing way. Our artists also share with you their favorite traditions or memories.

TELLING SANTA | By Stephanie McAtee

SANTA PAGE

1. Adhere a photo to red cardstock.

2. Rubber stamp journaling onto the photo with acrylic paint as your ink.

3. Fold book paper around the top and side of the layout and secure with staples.

4. Affix torn definitions to the photo.

5. Place a Page Pebble over part of a definition and secure a label holder over the top with staples.

6. Hang a chain of Washer Words, a photo and charm, connected with jump rings.

7. Place Alphabet Page Pebbles inside button covers and adhere to the layout with adhesive dots.

Alphabet page pebbles, jump rings, label holder, magnetic alphabet stamp, magnetic date stamp, staples and washer words: Making Memories
Alphabet stamps: PSX Design
Button covers: Dritz
Key charm: 7 Gypsies
Paint: Delta
Other: Book paper

My brother and I had a pact—whoever woke up first would crawl down the hallway to wake up the other, then we'd crawl past our parent's bedroom and down the hallway to the Christmas tree. If we got caught and sent back to bed, we would anxiously lay there until we thought our parents were *asleep*, then we'd try the journey again. Once we got to the Christmas tree, we plugged in the lights, dumped our stockings, and laid underneath the tree, eating our candy and checking out the gifts—all the time watching the clock until we could wake up our parents!

STEPHANIE McATEE

Angel

1. a messenger of God

3. one that is perfect, good and beautiful
2. CHARACTERIZED BY HAVING WINGS AND A HALO

JiLLiaN

ANGEL | BY JULIE TURNER

ANGEL PAGE

1. Apply a Simply Stated rub-on to white organdy paper.

2. Layer various sizes of paper, metal and fabric to create a background for your photo. Julie dry embossed the metal to create more texture.

3. Mount a photo to the top piece of paper.

4. Add mini eyelets to the right side of the photo.

5. Adhere a piece of twill tape near the bottom of the layout.

6. Cut apart a Defined sticker and heat emboss with embossing powder.

7. Affix one definition above the photo and affix the other two to a hinge. Attach the hinge over the twill tape. The hinge flips up to reveal more journaling.

8. Alter the Alphabet Charms by applying metallic rub-ons, pouring clear embossing powder on top and heat embossing.

9. Adhere the letters to the twill tape with adhesive dots.

Alphabet charms, defined sticker, eyelets, hinge, safety pin and simply stated rub-on: Making Memories
Embossing powder: Stampendous
Fabric: Waverly
Paper: Savoir
Pewter sheet metal: American Art Clay Co.
Stamping ink: Tsukineko
Other: Mulberry paper and twill tape

A few years ago we were surprised to find a can of pears and a note on our doorstep early on the morning of December 14th. We had no idea who left them, but there were new packages for the next 11 days, following the format of the *twelve* days of Christmas. Many of the items were silly, like bubble bath for swans-a-swimming or foot powder for lords-a-leaping. We never knew what to expect and tried all kinds of tactics to catch the gift-givers, but they were very sneaky. Finally, on Christmas Eve, the family revealed themselves to us and told us we were to carry on the tradition by doing the same for another family next year. We enjoyed it so much we've kept doing it every year!

JULIE TURNER

BELIEVE | By Kris Stanger

BELIEVE PAGE

1. Tea-dye canvas with regular tea bags and tea-dye the snap tape with Lipton Cold Brew tea bags to get a mustard color.

2. Ink the edges of the snap tape and mustard-colored cardstock with pigment ink.

3. Tape canvas to printer paper and print sheet music onto canvas.

4. Apply a Simply Stated rub-on to another piece of canvas.

5. Add snap tape to one side of the sheet music canvas.

6. Stitch around the canvas pieces with Scrapbook Stitches. Affix to the background paper.

7. String star Eyelet Charms on silk ribbon, tie knots at the ends and add to the layout.

8. Use a mini hinge on the journaling block to include more journaling on the page.

9. Tie fiber around the top of the photo to complete the layout.

Alphabet stamps: Hero Arts
Button: Dress It Up
Computer font: Bangle
Eyelet charms, mini hinge, scrapbook stitches and simply stated rub-ons: Making Memories
Fiber: On the Surface
Paper: Bazzill Basics and Provo Craft
Silk ribbon: Bucilla
Snap tape: Dritz
Stamping ink: Clearsnap
Other: Canvas and tea bags

Our most fun tradition is being visited by our family *elf* named Candy Cane. Every other Sunday beginning after Thanksgiving and lasting until Christmas Day, we are visited by Candy Cane. Our doorbell rings and at our door, we find brown bags with our children's names on them. The bags usually contain special holiday treats and a little note from Candy Cane. He lets the children know he has been watching them so he can report back to Santa. The last Sunday before Christmas, he leaves a special wooden toy or ornament. It is so fun to watch the kids react each time our doorbell rings during the holiday season!

KRIS STANGER

To me, a freshly-cut *tree* signals the beginning of the holiday season. Growing up, my family had the tradition of having a real tree in our house for the holidays. Ever since I married in 1994, I wanted to carry on the tradition of having a real tree in the house. There were times early on when we could barely afford to purchase gifts for each other, much less pay upwards of $50 for a tree that would "just get tossed to the curb" after the holidays (as Rigdon would point out). However, I've always insisted on my tree, and I'm happy to say it is now a solid Terrell family tradition.

ERIN TERRELL

PHOTO PAGE

1. Trim a ¼" from two sides of 12"x 12" paper. Mount on a background paper so you have a slight border.

2. Tear the top edge of a coordinating sheet of patterned paper, roll the torn edge, then rub with ink.

3. Mat your photos. On the double-matted photo, tear, roll and ink the bottom edge of the printed paper. Erin added pieces of vellum at various places under the photos for added color and interest.

4. Affix the matted photos to the background page.

5. Add strips of green cardstock and embellish with rick rack and loosely-knotted ribbon. Erin rubbed copper ink over the green cardstock for more contrast.

6. To alter the Alphabet Charms, apply metallic rub-ons with your finger.

7. Pour clear embossing powder on top and heat emboss.

8. Adhere to your layout with adhesive dots.

9. Apply a Simply Stated rub-on to one photo and add a matted Defined sticker to another photo.

Alphabet charms, defined stickers and simply stated rub-on: Making Memories
Embossing powder: Stampendous
Metallic rub-ons: Craf-T Products
Paper: Colors By Design and Daisy D's
Pen: EK Success
Ribbon: Best Value
Stamping ink: Inkadinkado and Tsukineko
Vellum: K & Company
Other: Rick rack

2002 CHRISTMAS CARD PHOTOS | BY ERIN TERRELL

A MERRY CHRISTMAS | By Robin Johnson

MERRY CHRISTMAS PAGE

1. Cut out the center of patterned paper and zig zag stitch to cardstock.

2. Cut strips of coordinating paper to block in the photo area.

3. Glue rick rack across the top edge of the bottom block and add Eyelet Shapes to the ends. To change the color of Eyelet Shapes, hold with tweezers and apply gold metallic rub-ons to the top. Heat emboss with clear embossing powder.

4. For the tags and photo corners, stamp words or write a title where desired. Brush the edges with an ink pad. Cover with clear ink and heat emboss with embossing enamel.

5. For the flower, punch two shapes from cardstock. Ink with clear ink, cover with embossing enamel and heat-set. Offset the shapes and glue together. Add gold beads for the center.

Beads: Designs by Pamela
Embossing enamel: Ultra Thick Embossing
Embossing powder: Stampendous
Enamel, Suze Weinberg
Eyelet shapes: Making Memories
Flower punch: EK Success
Paper: Making Memories, Anna Griffin and Printworks
Rick rack: Wrights
Stamping ink: Tsukineko
Tags: Avery
Other: Ribbon and script rubber stamp

Christmas is the perfect time to remember loved ones. But what if a special loved one is no longer living? In our home, we found a meaningful way to *honor* those we miss during the holidays. We choose a worthy charity and donate in his or her name. Next, we write a letter noting the name of the charity and the gift given. We also record a favorite memory of that person. Finally, the letter is placed among the branches of the Christmas tree so we can think of that person throughout the holiday season. The letters are kept each year and stored in a scrapbook.

ROBIN JOHNSON

Throughout my childhood, I remember spending

Christmas day with all my relatives who lived in

Arizona. We always went to my grandparents'

house, and it was constantly noisy, exciting, fun

and full of hustle and bustle! One year, however,

we added a new tradition. On Christmas Eve, just

my immediate family gathered in the living room

around the Christmas tree. We sang Christmas

songs, my father *read* the story of

Christ's birth from the New Testament and my

younger siblings acted out the Nativity scene.

Afterwards, we exchanged the gifts we had for

each other. It was wonderful having this time

together, just the seven of us. I still honor this

tradition with my own family.

SHARON LEWIS

SOPHIE'S PAGE

1. Tear a piece of sheet music to create a vertical page border.

2. Trim two patterned papers and color block the rest of the background paper.

3. Double mat a photo, tearing the top and bottom edges of the mat. Add Charmed Photo Corners to the photo.

4. Wrap a scrap of velvet around the left side of the page and machine stitch in place.

5. Ink the edges of the background paper, tag and in between the sheet music and patterned papers.

6. With an X-Acto knife and ruler, cut slits in the background paper for the ribbon to slide through.

7. Slide ribbon through the slits and add Ribbon Charms and tie bows/knots. Attach the tag Eyelet Charm with a jump ring.

8. Decorate a tag with Alphabet Page Pebbles, Defined stickers, torn sheet music, and alphabet stamps. Affix the tag to the bottom strip of paper.

Alphabet page pebbles, charmed photo corners, defined sticker, eyelet charm and ribbon charms: Making Memories
Alphabet stamps: PSX Design
Paper: Making Memories, Anna Griffin and Karen Foster Design
Stamping ink: Clearsnap
Tag: Avery
Other: Handmade paper, ribbon, sheet music and velvet

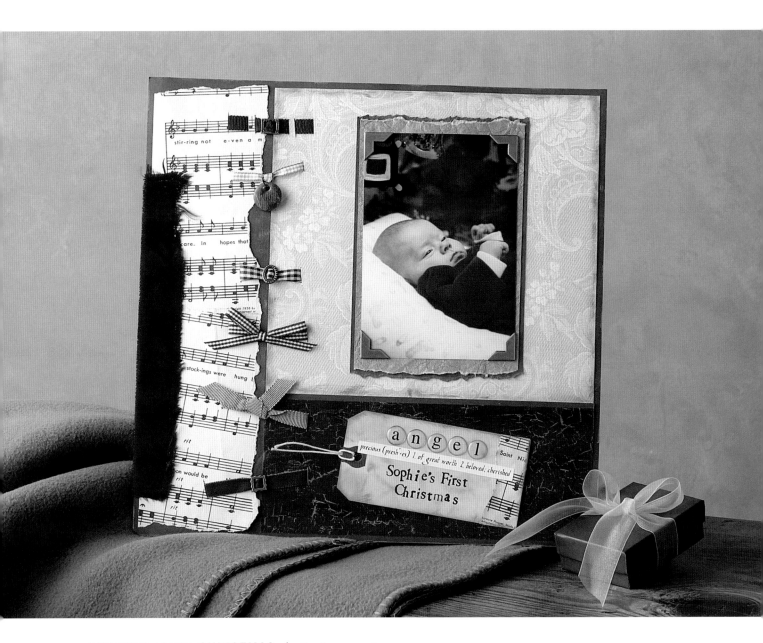

SOPHIE'S FIRST CHRISTMAS | By Sharon Lewis

CHRISTMAS MAGIC | By Heidi Swapp

MAGIC PAGE

1. Trace a circle from a dinner plate.

2. Select the photos you want to use, then determine the size of window that will accommodate the photos.

3. Cut out the circle, then cut out the window in the wheel.

4. Determine where you will place the wheel. Heidi's hung over the top just a bit so the viewer can operate the wheel from a top-loading sheet protector.

5. Find the middle of the circle and poke a hole for your brad.

6. Determine where you would like the wheel mounted on cardstock. Poke a hole there, too.

7. Position the photos under the wheel. It may take some rearranging to get them under the wheel just right. Heidi positioned hers so they are always oriented in the same direction.

8. Once the photos are in place, attach the wheel with a brad on top of a Washer Word.

9. Embellish the circle with old postcards, Charmed Photo Corners, Alphabet charms, book paper, alphabet stamps and other assorted ephemera.

10. Wrap walnut-inked tags around the left side of the layout.

Alphabet stamps: PSX Design
Alphabet charms, brads, charmed photo corners, ribbon, ribbon charm, staples and washer word: Making Memories
Tags: Avery
Walnut ink: Postmodern Design
Other: Book paper, ephemera, foam stamp and large alphabet stamps

My grandpa Kasteler used to hand make his Christmas *cards* every year. He attended art school in California and had learned creative printing techniques. He also had a real knack for rhyme. Each year he got the whole family involved in production, and usually 250 cards later, he created the most innovative and inspiring things I have ever seen. I love hearing the stories from my dad about Grandpa carving a linoleum block and stamping each card with three different colors or when he took extra shingles from their new home and created their holiday greetings on that! Several years ago, my aunt KJ compiled copies from each year and gave to each of us grandkids. What a treasure! I find that the thing I look forward to most every year is creating our family Christmas card.

HEIDI SWAPP

Every year when I was growing up, my mom would

buy or make each of us kids a Christmas ornament.

The *ornament* was always

representative of us at that time, whether it was

a hobby we were interested in or an activity at

school in which we were involved. One year, for

example, my mom bought a doll ornament and

remade the clothes to look like my cheerleading

uniform. It's been fun to look through my personal

ornaments and reminisce of years past. I've carried

on this tradition with my own children, and I find

them so excited to get out their personal box of

ornaments and help trim the tree.

LYNNE MONTGOMERY

TRADITION PAGE

1. Adhere a patterned lace panel to Perspectives paper with spray adhesive.

2. Spread a thin layer of modeling paste over the material so the texture of the material shows through. Allow to dry.

3. Trim the fabric edges and cut material away from the Perspective openings. Add photos behind the openings.

4. Apply a Simply Stated rub-on over the photos.

5. Print your journaling on a sheet of regular paper. Hold the paper up to a light source and center tags over the paper with adhesive tabs. Feed the paper through the back of your printer (so it remains flat) to print the words on the tags.

6. Create a strip of paper using the same technique used to create the background. You could also use a ribbon strip.

7. Mount Alphabet Charms on the strip with pop-dots.

8. Hang the printed tags around the pop-dots with linen thread and beaded jump rings.

9. Attach the embellished strip with nickel rectangles, snaps and plaid ribbon.

---

*Alphabet charms, jump rings, metal-rimmed
tags, simply stated rub-ons and snaps:
Making Memories
Computer font: Teletype
Jewelry tags: American Tag Co.
Modeling paste: Liquitex
Nickel rectangles: 7 Gypsies
Paper: Perspectives, Making Memories
Other: Beads, lace panel, linen thread and ribbon*

TRADITION | By Lynne Montgomery

THREE QUESTIONS FOR SANTA | By Jennifer Jensen

QUESTIONS PAGE

1. Frame a sepia-tone photo with an old photo mat. Wrap ribbon around the mat.

2. Mount photo on black paper and add lace under the bottom of the matted photo.

3. Decorate a tag with buttons, ribbon, rick rack and other found objects.

4. Jennifer photocopied Addison's hand-written note to Santa and questions she wanted to ask him, then used that for the journaling.

Adhesive: Mod Podge, Plaid
Alphabet stickers: Nostalgiques, EK Success
Jump rings: Making Memories
Paper: Anna Griffin and Paper Adventures
Other: Bell, buckles, buttons, fabric, holly leaf, lace, old frame, ribbon, rick rack, safety pin and upholstery tacks

Every December 23rd, we have a family gathering with whoever happens to be in town for the holidays. After a delicious dinner, we listen for the fabulous moment we've waited for all year long. At first it's very faint, then as that one person approaches our porch, the jingling becomes ever so clear and the "Ho Ho Ho, Merry Christmas" definitely gives it away! He arrives after dark and always has his red velvet bag trimmed with large silver jingle bells. Each child gets a turn on his lap and receives a special gift. When every child has had a turn, *santa* grabs a quick snack, then he's back to work to get ready for the big event. We look forward to his visit every year!

JENNIFER JENSEN

TRADITIONS | By Emily Waters

TRADITIONS PAGE

1. Dry brush cream paint over the background paper. Sand off any excess.

2. Scan old postcards and print onto cream-colored cardstock. Brush with walnut ink for an aged look.

3. Tear a strip of the postcards and sew it to the left side of the left-hand page.

4. Attach red ribbon down the left side with screw snaps.

5. Brush Charmed Frames with red acrylic paint, making sure paint is in all grooves. Wipe off excess paint using a paper towel or baby wipe, making sure to leave paint in crevices.

6. Add photos to the frames and adhere down the side of the page.

7. Attach a Defined sticker to the layout and wrap a small piece of ribbon around it.

8. Tear another section of postcard paper and attach on the bottom corner. Leave the top open to form a pocket.

9. Embellish the layout with Simply Stated rub-ons, Defined stickers and torn cardstock.

10. Attach photos in desired places with brads or stitched photo corners.

Brads, charmed frames, defined stickers, simply stated rub-ons, staples and snaps:
Making Memories
Paint: Delta
Paper: Bazzill Basics
Other: Ribbon

While growing up, we had many traditions in our home, but the one that stands out the most is the one that reminded us about the true meaning of Christmas. Each morning right after breakfast, starting on December 1st, we would gather in our family room—hot chocolate in hand—and listen to my mom read a special *story*. Each story was a little reminder of what Christmas is all about and that it is a season of giving. Each day the story was different, but the meaning was the same. After the story, we would all leave home, each going in a different direction, with a reminder of what is most important during the holiday season. I have kept a record of all of the stories and hope to pass on the tradition to my children someday.

EMILY WATERS

With a big extended family, it can become quite

expensive to give a gift to each cousin or even to

each family. To remedy this problem, my mom's

side of the family started an ornament exchange.

A year prior, we randomly select a name and

purchase or make an ornament for that person.

Then every Thanksgiving, we get together and

exchange ornaments. It's fun selecting an

ornament to represent

that person's accomplishment or interest that

particular year. And it's fun to decorate our tree

with the ornaments we've received over the years.

ERIN TRIMBLE

HOLIDAY PAGE

1. Back two Perspective openings with red cardstock. Back the center opening with black.

2. Create two accordion-fold books. Embellish, then attach to the red cardstock. Place a length of Scrapbook Stitches behind each book to tie closed.

3. Rub the Charmed Plaque with rub-ons, cover with embossing and heat emboss.

4. Add page corner, journaling, photos and ribbon.

Alphabet stamps: PSX Design
Charmed plaque and scrapbook stitches:
Making Memories
Computer fonts: Earwig Factory, Hootie and
John Doe, downloaded from the Internet;
2Peas Billboard and 2Peas Flea Market,
downloaded from www.twopeasinabucket.com;
CK Windsong, Creating Keepsakes
Embossing enamel: Ultra Thick Embossing
Enamel, Suze Weinberg
Metallic rub-ons: Craf-T Products
Paper: Perspectives, Making Memories
Stamping ink: Clearsnap
Other: Date stamp and ribbon

Besides seeing *Eliza* get excited about CHRISTMAS, we love Christmas for many reasons. Here are our **TOP 20** reasons why it is

our

favorite

holiday

OUR FAVORITE HOLIDAY | By Erin Trimble

A childhood tradition I remember vividly is decorating gingerbread houses. My mom would spend days making the houses, then they would sit for a day or two so the icing could harden. Part of the fun was pouring over magazines and Christmas books to decide what we would tackle that year. And for two to three months before Christmas, we would be on search for the most unusual *candy* to decorate our masterpieces! Our gingerbread houses formed the perfect city. My mom would put them on a table that had lights and batting (to simulate snow). Now that I am a mom, I have a new respect for the work my mom put into all of that.

RHONDA SOLOMON

CHRISTMAS TREE PAGE

1. Cut a square in the middle of green cardstock.

2. Attach screen to the back of the cardstock opening with eyelets.

3. Tie ribbon and jute through eyelets.

4. Make fabric-covered buttons following manufacturer's directions.

5. Stitch buttons onto the page with a needle and thread.

6. Print journaling on fabric and machine stitch to the background.

7. To make the typewriter letters, rubber stamp letters onto printed paper, cut out with a circle punch and mat on coordinating cardstock.

8. Frame letters with old typewriter key frames and fill with Diamond Glaze.

9. Ink the edges of the matted letters and the edges of the background paper.

10. Rubber stamp an "O" onto fabric and trim with pinking sheers.

11. For the word "tree," stamp a background stamp on red cardstock with white ink. Rubber stamp the word "tree." Trim with pinking sheers. Mat with fabric.

12. Write "O Christmas tree" on white cardstock and stitch to layout.

13. Attach red printed paper behind the screen.

14. Secure a photo to the screen with ribbon and a Ribbon Charm.

Adhesive: Diamond Glaze, JudiKins
Alphabet stamps: The Missing Link
Stamping Company
Button-covering kit: Dritz
Charmed plaque and ribbon charms:
Making Memories
Typewriter key frames: Coffee Break Design
Other: Fabric, jute, ribbon and screen

We start talking to Dad about the tree right after turkey dinner. He starts to roll his eyes and make funny sounds but after my mom gives him a look he agrees. This year we put the big tree boxes on the front of Dad's jeep and we drove up to the front door. We are a very big help to Dad the day the tree goes up.

O CHRISTMAS TREE | By Rhonda Solomon

be inspired.™

In A SEASON OF GIVING, our artists give a bit of themselves by offering inspiring ideas for all aspects of the Christmas season. Discover new ways you can give of yourself and add more joy and merriment to your holidays.

HOME DÉCOR | ORNAMENTS | HOMEMADE GIFTS | NEIGHBOR GIFTS

HOLIDAY PARTIES | GIFTS CHILDREN CAN MAKE | ADVENT CALENDARS

TAGS & WRAPPING | CARDS & CARD HOLDERS | SCRAPBOOK PAGES

ITEM# 23370

ISBN 1-893352-23-4

6 04062 23370 5

9 781893 352230

$19.99 U.S.

makingm